12-12-12

THE CRIES BEHIND THE BARS

BY ANGIE RICHARDSON
(AKA)
"ANGIESAIDTHAT"

1

Self Published: Angela Richardson
Cover designed by Newport Prison inmate

Disclaimer:
The names of some of the characters have been changed to protect
 The rights and privacy of the individuals referenced. Furthermore,
The opinions and statements expressed are solely the opinions of
The author.

PRINTED IN THE UNITED STATES OF AMERICA

Dedication

This book is dedicated to my Mother, Elaine Richardson and Mrs. Washington,   may you both Rest in Peace and Love.

I must give all praises to My Creator and his son, Jesus Christ.   Without the two of these Higher Powers I would be non-existing.   I can't lie like I am a Holy Ghost Christian.   But I am a work in progress and in touch with me Spiritual Creator.

Acknowledgement

As I continue to press down on my pen trying to hold back the tears on this part, I know these people believed in me even after the 12-12-12 nightmare.   They understood my addiction for gambling and each one of them knows my heart and that I am gifted and talented.

My oldest sister, Sharon, Doll Baby, you are one of the world's greatest sister.   To hear you cry when my verdict was read and for the judge to have you escorted out of the courtroom made me feel some type of way. He's doing a job that allows him to "get paid regardless" while battling an addiction of his own.   Some you expect to understand and some you don't.   Hey, remember when you dropped me out of the red wagon as a child?   My head has finally healed.   My life finally makes sense.   I love you truly!

AngieSaidThat

Kim Hughes, girl, you have truly been a ride or die friend/sister! I appreciate all the scriptures, quotes, letters, money, and the overall love and support.   I appreciate you believing in the AngieSaidThat comeback after the hurricane verdict.   And that ain't no bullshit!

I love you!

LaShon Mosely, you are the truth!   Thanks for all the money, love, cards, calls, and prayers.   Do you want it, huh?

Love,

AngieSaidThat

Keacie, I know you were going through the hardest time in your life to survive breast cancer.   To have your spiritual friend/ex-lover/sister (all running con-current) talk you through the painful heartache of slowly watching your mother die of cancer.   GOD allowed me to keep her laughing and taking a pain pill with her to make it easier just to know someone like myself did not want her in pain.   The fact of bathing her, eating strawberries with her, and liking Face book pictures with her are priceless memories.   Even that Friday when my Public Defender called saying I had a warrant for my arrest and my bond had been revoked, it was worth avoiding the police because she needed to holla @ ha' boy!
(RIP Ma) Mrs. Washington

Love always, Angiesaidthat

Vona Cox, "*I want to go outside in the rain, so nobody will see me crying.*" It was your powerful text message that changed my life and now you are reading it!   To be honest, you helped me seekmy Creator and ask him to reveal my purpose.   I can't express in words how thankful I am to have a friend like you in my life.   So, how about a pair of jeans with your name on it worn by AngieSaidThat!   Thank you so much for the text that helped me to find my purpose.

Love always,
Angie

I've been told as a great comedian and as a headliner you save the best for last.

      My Wife, you created the name "AngieSaidThat" on my   Face book page. Most likely, I said that! Most say it is not the Christian way to love the same sex. The State of Arkansas passed the same sex marriage law and a few days later they took it back. Believe me President Obama, Judge Piazza, and Judge Gray supports our love. GOD knows the heart of it all. Even if I have to order you a ponytail holder from commissary you will have a band. It may be a rubber band or a plastic band, but the love is what's inside of it. I'm ma put a ring on it!

I love you!

Angie

Introduction

Angela Richardson is 44 years old and from Little Rock, Arkansas. The most popular lesbiana (Spanish for lesbian) in the state. The only black gay club owner in the state of Arkansas and is sentenced to twenty-one years in prison. She introduces readers to an entirely new kind of slavery. A slavery that has no color. Her joyful spirit was overtaken by a gambling addiction. She was weakened by the love of shooting dice. She finally found healing from her addiction through writing.

A text message from a long time friend in Atlanta, GA, by the name of Vona Cox, changed her life by asking her the simply question. "What is your purpose in life?" Struggling with understanding the question, AngieSaidThat, really couldn't reply.

On June 4, 2014, a jury verdict changed her life. The security guard lied with a strange and most surprising plot twist over a gap in teeth caused her to be sentenced unfairly and unjustly to twenty-one years in prison for being the driver in a bank robbery.

The Little Rock Police was told by an informant, who is also a police impersonator which flashes a blue police light to pull over young men and have oral sex with them, that it was I and my security guard that robbed the bank. The police impersonation was reported to a Little Police Sergeant and of course no action was ever taken.

The truth of the matter is after healing from her gambling addiction and discovering her purpose and passion for writing, she now realizes just how amazing she really is!

I could see my struggle wondering how long it is going to last. A gambling addiction had gone bad.

12-12-12 like Satan got in my ear. "Let's go gamble my dear."
Driving the car is what I agreed to do.

A few months later, I prayed heavy for a cure. Not understanding the
law, twenty-one years hit me in the jaw. The punishment I can bear, the
years are unjustified and unfair. (No gun, no prior convictions, having a
gap damn near got me sentenced to the electric chair by a jury that was
not of my homosexual peers caused me later tears.)

I'm not the person I used to be, chasing dice. Newport Prison can't
even serve ice. I am redeemed so set me free; reduce my time,
reconsideration of one's mind. Allow me to shake of these prison
chains, stop the pain and wipe away the tear stains.

The blessing of this black ink has caused me to think, writing with
creative skills gives my spirits chills. I save my thoughts for now, it
gets better later. Enjoy my book like a pack of Now & Later. My two
buck teeth remind my friend Shon of the Bugs Bunny, except this is not
funny.

That ain't all folks. Marty's attorney knows about the guy with the gap.
This reminds me of Brokeback Mountain for real. Even the one with
the gun got a better deal! Is this justice served for real? The informant
pretending to be a cop, they all enjoyed men being on top and the
ex-judge well, he liked dipping the "thug chocolate fudge".

AngieSaidThat

Chapter 1

"The Cries Behind the Bars"
June 8, 2014

Now that I am currently behind bars without any material possessions, but wealthy in spirits of faith and hope, I am in deep thoughts about my complicated life as I sat behind the bars on aggravated robbery charges. Whenever you do not know your purpose in life you sometimes find out that your life doesn't even make sense. And what does age have to do with it? At forty-three years old I found out, nothing! I later realized that I was a mentor to an entire community. My entire life took a turn that I really did not see coming on 12-12-12. I battled an out of control gambling addiction. I never denied the fact that it had me. I also had a learning disability that I was dealing as well, funny enough with my personality others overlooked it. I dressed very well keeping my appearances on point. I am a very well known, popular, and good looking person. I find it hard to believe a gap in my teeth got me convicted, but that is what's reported in the newspaper article.

I started off hosting at Backstreet Night Club years ago. Later, after knowing that the owner really didn't care for black people, I decided to start hosting parties to allow everyone to dress and express themselves.

In 2000, I lost the most important person in my life to cancer. My hero, my mother, Elaine Richardson, she was my everything. I wanted to die. I no longer cared about life itself. Behind all the hurt and pain my life took a turn. I found a cure for it all, shooting dice everyday with the high Rollers. I couldn't make it a day without shooting craps. I needed to see a seven or eleven on the first roll. Winner, winner, chicken dinner! I needed gambling like some people needed crack.

~ 12-12-12 ~

Sometimes, people say if you're going to do anything it's best to do it by yourself. Sometimes you can't let your right hand know what the left hand is doing. I am beginning to believe it's true.

I can honestly speak about it now but, after almost two years of being free on bond, my healing process kicked in. My life took a turn through writing a book titled "Unfiltered". The book actually got my spirit closer to my Creator. I changed my surrounding of people. What really happens when certain friends and family are turned away and life seems like it's never ending.

I had to deal with myself. I became my worst enemy. Very hostile towards myself. I am now my best friend. I had five cars of my choice. At one point I saved almost $7,000.00 in two months. All bills paid from hosting events and later able to open my own night club.

I now realize that I was the "nitch" or some say a blessing to a community. Now I sit in jail writing to apologize to those that still admire me and that I have let down.   This book expresses my words of wisdom.   I'm not Sorry for the things I truly shared with the youth.   It's the truth, the fact of my hidden secrets.   It is so much easier to talk about others situation versus your very own.

With hope, faith, and prayer, I still feel as if I have it all.   I know my Creator is here with me as I share my stories and move my books with my purpose.   I have prayed over each story and even my very own. There are so many readers behind the bars and all I can vision is "AngieSaidThat" books being distributed and the people craving to read them.   I am focused on writing a series about it all.

The story of my incarceration actually begins like this.   It was a Wednesday morning.   I got a call from one of the security guards that worked for me at the club.   I had the only black alternative nightclub in Little Rock, Arkansas, better known as a black gay club.

Marty called and said, "Hey, I need to go hit a lick.   I need to get my hands on some quick money."   I knew I had gambled a large amount of money for the entire month and it was My Wife's birthday.   She really wasn't the type of woman that required material things in life.   I just wanted to go gamble.   I figured it would be quick and easy and I also wanted to make up for my losses, so I decided to take a chance and go hit the lick.   The three of us discussed it and pulled it off, but I wasn't inside the bank.   To be honest, I never mentioned anyone's name to the detectives, not even to this day.   I also feel as if everyone involved had committed a crime at some point in their lives.   It's just Some don't get caught.   However, if you do you have to pay the price.   We also have those that are called "snitches" and will do whatever it takes to save their own skin.   They are innocent once it's time to face the judge and they played no part, they just know about it.

Marty is a heavy set black male and had a problem with the truth about it all.   I felt like he would break down and tell, but I never turned my back on him the entire time he sat in jail until he continued lying about how I threatened his mother and sent him money to keep quiet. All of it was so untrue. Lies. He did just what the prosecutor wanted him to do. Lie. All of a sudden he claims I'm the mastermind of it all, but didn't reveal his ex-boyfriend. I admit that no one could even identify the female in the bank. It took for him to say who was actually with him. It's also the same way if you are selling drugs, somehow, some way your friend, associate, or partner will eventually give your name up. So tell me this; his boyfriend also had a gap, but did the jury dislike homosexuals? What is the meaning of this logic to you?

I confessed my sins to my Creator and repented. In the midst of all of this, my mind is continuously going through a healing process. While out on bond for almost two years and even before being convicted on an aggravated robbery charge my mind and my spirit were healing. The most positive change; I stopped shooting dice. I changed my surroundings. But I still had to deal with what happened on 12-12-12. I wanted all those 12s to just go away. My book that I took time to write titled "Unfiltered" brought me out of my own fear factors, sadness, and depression. It actually gave me hope. It was simply therapeutic to my mind. I wanted to start my life over again. I never saw imprisonment coming my way. During my addiction stage, I really didn't care. I really didn't understand my purpose in life. I can't even say that I had a purpose. Do I now?

So many people predicted the world would come to an end in 2012. The only person's world that came to an end was mine. The ending of a demon that was very disappointed when he was no longer able to destroy me with a gambling addiction. I am the truth. Now that my spirit is working in favor with GOD, I am now able to represent my Creator. I got a special visit from Brother Paul, the pastor of Friendly Chapel Church. He is such a great man. I visited his church a few years ago with a long time friend of mine name Vee. He truly has a loving, honest, and respectable sweet heart. Brother Paul is in his late fifties or early sixties, salt & pepper hair and is a great white man that never judges anyone. He will help save your soul. I am really thankful that he even remembered me, but I'm not someone easily forgotten.

Two weeks after sitting in jail facing twenty-one years, I didn't have my hopes up too high on an appeal or hope for a reduced

sentencing.   But, I knew I wasn't going to give up on writing the judge, senator, mayor, or anyone to get my sentence reduced because it was unfair.   I never owned a gun and surely if Marty, the suspect shown in the video with a gun, already on probation with three other gun charges could get   his charge dropped down to robbery, how
Is that justice was fairly served to me? Why are my charges so extreme?

I noticed a lot of young black females from the LGBT community are here on various charges.   Everyone knows me from being so popular in the diversity community.   I stood up for the black gay community when no one else had the nerves to do so.   I didn't have a team.   It was just me.   I raised money for those in need of it.   For those with AIDS, season greetings, pageants, and more.   I battled a gambling addiction and several personalities.

Now all I can hear is other inmates talking through the toilets. Screaming all day "I need a flush" and hoping either one of the inmates or guards would eventually come and push the silver button outside the door that controls the toilet inside the cell.   I instantly got sick in my stomach due to the fact that my cellmate Justice had enjoyed all of the beans, eggs, oatmeal, mac and cheese, and the strong black coffee.   So you can only imagine what type of waste management she had to release. "Code Red", meaning medical.   I lay on the top bunk and placed one of my white T-shirts over my nose.   I rubbed it down with Irish Spring soap.   I would take a deep breath as needed to get past the smell.   I made sure the few times we were able to get out for one hour in the morning and one hour in the evening to find time for working out, trying to stomach the vegetables or the dog chow trays,   And made sure I didn't drink anything but water.   I prayed that my body had a better chance along with the vitamins I ordered off the commissary list that has yet to be in stock.   I would get oranges from the younger inmates that loved my Personality.   Every Tuesday, they called those who ordered commissary.   It is truly a blessing to have people on the outside to even care enough to put money on your books.   The prices on the list were expensive to be locked up.   It is much cheaper on the outside, but we all know the state has a way to keep getting money.   We must pay for our privileges even in jail.

Justice, my cellmate, had been in and out of jail, and even to prison before.   She battled back and forth on drugs.   Most days I totally blocked her out of my mind to focus on writing.   She talked until she started snoring and that didn't make it any better.   I did whatever I could to get out of the cell.   Every day the guards picked inmates and gave them chances to be on clean-up.   I got picked sometimes to give out ice or pick up trays after eating just to get out of the cell.

To have only been in here two weeks and facing twenty-one years I wanted to die at times, but I knew without a doubt I didn't have the nerves to attempt a suicide move.   My only way to cope is with prayer, faith and exercise.   I enjoyed writing.   They allowed us one very small pencil and I ordered a dictionary and three 8.5 X 11 writing pads from the commissary list.   The phone cards cost ten dollars per card @ .25 cents per minute with only a 40 minute limit.   The life of a prisoner wasn't the life GOD planned for me.   An addiction of any kind will have you in situations that only GOD can help you out of by touching the right people to allow different movements to happen. Yeeesss!

Out of all the books to read along with the Bible, my cellmate walked in with a book the truly got my attention, "Mentor: The Kid & The CEO" by Tom Pace with Walter Jenkins.   I encourage everyone to read it.   I got so caught up into the book that I didn't want the book to end.   I thought to myself how the main character, Malcolm, played such a great impact in Tony's life at a time when he really needed guidance.   I lay in the top bunk searching the book for an address to write Tom Pace, but the contact information available was only an e-mail address.   Well, that was out for me being inside a jail cell

I heard things were different in prison and you are able to enroll in different programs.   I really had no time to waste.   At this time things were on a daily routine with me.   I couldn't do much, but I had to set my mind on my purpose, His purpose, any purpose.

I didn't want any of the younger generation to think it was cool to do drugs, get high, bully people, steal, kill, nor destroy. It is not right nor is it cool and any addiction of any kind will destroy you and your character if you don't get a hold of it in a timely and respectful manner.

I had a few guards to ask me if I was famous due to the fact so many people knew me. I have so many regrets, but my faith and hope will allow me to help others to avoid making wrong decisions. It is not worth it! Life is so much more than getting up every shift for standing head count, waiting for someone to flush your toilet, watching others come back and forth to jail and prison. We all have a purpose in life and you can conquer any destiny with hope!

I can't promise you that it will be easy, but there's a rainbow behind every cloud, as quoted by Oprah Winfrey.

The reason I'm so sure of my time being cut short and my writing skills making worldwide movements after only two weeks and facing twenty-one years is because GOD has assured me that there are people that represent him while others think they have all the power. I do believe in punishment. I just don't think anyone should be treated unfairly. I just wasn't advised properly. Bottom line...I was misrepresented.

I have taken out the time to write the judge regarding overturning my sentencing. I prayed hard and to be honest I have been told not to put all your trust in "the man". The only thing I know remains the same is a tree. We all know every year a tree has four changing seasons, summer, fall, winter and spring. Therefore, anything else is capable of change. I picked up this small pencil and didn't even care if blisters formed over my entire hand. I had to continue to allow my name, " AngieSaidThat", to touch others in a way that my Creator would be proud of the fact he shows me favor.

I heard about the big headline in the newspaper article written about me as if I was running for president, but I didn't care about the negativity.   My mind knew that the media and others would want to get to know me.   I am not the monster the prosecutors made me out to be. They have a job to do.   It is the newspaper's job to report what happened, not what they feel   happened.

June 3rd & 4th, 2014

~ The State Of Arkansas vs Angela Richardson ~

A few days before the trial there was a warrant issued for my arrest for threatening a witness.   Simply a lie.   This dude, Jo-Jo, was involved at one point with Marty, until they started cheating with some of the same guys in the gay community.   Jo-Jo claimed I threatened him and that my niece broke out his window.   I was arrested on something I simply had no clue about ever happening.   I am not the writer that makes up stories.   I

speak on realness.   I honestly feel like everyone has "A Story To Tell", which is the very first book I wrote in 2004, but my immature mind wasn't ready for the journey.   I am focused now and writing with a purpose!
I'm so thankful that Tom Pace made it his business to make sure his books were placed in jails.   Well needed and much appreciated.   I complained about the prices of the phone cards, but it was a blessing to find a contact phone number for Tom Pace.   I only had a few minutes remaining on my card and by all means I called the long distance number trying to get an address to write. I got the voicemail on my first try and with excitement listened to Tom Pace's voice.

I made sure while others wanted to smoke, watch TV, gossip or whatever they chose to do on activity time that I was going to make calls, read, write, exercise, and pray.

It was no other way I could do this time without keeping the commitments I listed above.   However, living the lifestyle of a lesbian at a time like this all the women locked up is willing to experience some type of relationship with the same sex.   I have no desire whatsoever!

True enough with my name letters and messages started coming to me before I could realize this was really happening to me. I had been numb during the two days of trial listening to so many lies being told by deceitful people that I've helped out of the goodness of my heart. Do I regret the fact I've helped so many? No. Since I have been here I have taken the time to talk to the younger females that have cases facing a lot of time.

I explained that my life changed on 12-12-12 and that it has caused me to be facing twenty-one years in prison. I tell them that I am now focused on the why's and why not of life. Hopefully, I can talk them into reading and praying. I am not going to force anything on anyone including my homosexual lifestyle. I stay away from those women that are trying t o get close to me on that level. I am currently with a very special person. I am not sure if she is going to stick this time out with me or not, but I will definitely try to do what Malcolm did in a time of thunderstorm to renew my commitment. I want to be loyal to her. First of all I want to be loyal to my Creator and to myself overall. He knows my heart and that is what matters most.

I have placed my laundry towel on the hard iron steel stool in order to continue writing. Every minute of the hour all I hear is beating on the walls, "I need a flush", or "Someone pass me a smoke." I find myself praying even harder to make others laugh when I really want to cry myself. I can't worry myself about what the next day is going to bring. I deal with today's challenges through prayer, mindful thoughts, and exercising.

I advise anyone to read now. I hated reading but after reading Tom Pace's book I promised myself I would read a book at least once a week. I enjoyed writing, but hated reading. Its days like this you feel so helpless. You want to give up on your dreams, life accomplishments, and even prayers. You know not to question GOD, but find yourself with your hands up searching for answers. All I can think about are my twin nieces and wanting to build a positive relationship with them. I am so thankful that I stayed on my nephew, Adrienne, about staying out of trouble, always practicing safe sex, and to be the best he can possible be in the Air Force. I wanted him to travel the world and be a respectable grown man. I told him to keep GOD in his life and everything would work out in his favor. I helped to raise him and he is my heart. There are a lot of lives that I have made a very strong impact on. Once I get this time reduced I will again touch the lives of others in a most positive way for sure! So many people tell me I will be locked up for the next twelve years. True enough even the judge knows my sentencing was unfair. Without being able to afford a paid attorney is this what you deserve in a court appointed public defender? Are you even advised fairly? When you simply don't know, who do you turn to? It was ineffective counsel.

As I sat in my cell and looked over the commissary list I noticed at the bottom it stated don't forget to check out the fresh favorite Friday. You get the privilege to see a list with both cheeseburgers and fries or chicken nuggets or the menu is subject to change to a slice of cheese pizza for $6.00 per order. I wasn't to big on eating a lot, just small portion of meals a day really helped me out versus watching my cellmate, Justice. She ate my tray and hers. She still wanted almost half of everything I had from commissary. She never offered me any of whatever she did get a hold of. It's just some things in here I was not about to accept nor adjust to.

Justice was a very funny person. She told me that she got approved for her social security check by placing a small bag in the back of her panties sealed with a small piece of tape. As she was being interviewed she made herself cough and fart. Inside the bag was peanut butter, honey, corn and chocolate syrup. She explained to the representative that she had made a mess in her clothes and stuck her hand inside her panties and started licking her fingers! Approved! The first few times she explained to me before her drug addiction how she modeled as the Wendy's girl with the nice costume and curly red yarn hair. I looked at her head and told her when she got out maybe she could do a commercial for McDonald's. Her hair, oily braids was very thin and blond and reminded me of stringy fries…low calories.

I know that I am the only one in here able to deal with Justice. She had other cellmates, but they kicked on The door screaming how they had to get out the room. My numbness and spirit stepped and listened to her complaints, screaming through the door all that she had gone through starting at the age of twelve. From being raped, to being a runway model and ending up with a crack addiction. I openly tell her story in my book "Unfiltered" as I continue with the cries behind the bars.

Chapter 2

My LGBT & Church Members

I've stood in front of the State Capital with Judge Gray and The Care Organization to speak out about equality. I have mentored the youth at the Job Corp Center speaking on judgment and equality. The person the prosecutors spoke against on June 3rd & 4th, 2014 have been destroyed forever. I rebuke 12-12-12 in the name of Jesus. That's the date it happened and that's how many years they claim it will be before I am eligible for parole. Just watch Jesus work this all out!

The devil felt disrespected because he could no longer use me and let those who had formed against me attack me in the midst of it all. I will return again. The enemy shall be placed under my footsteps. I have consumed them by finding my purpose in life. I will continue to write and help others. I will stick to my daily routine of things. I will become one of the best writers yet. AngieSaidThat

I stopped going to church.   Personally I found a church that I really enjoyed the preaching and the teaching of the Words of GOD. Some pastors are so stuck on living the rich and famous life.   GOD has ways of showing a person that he is not to be played with or taken for granted.   At one point in my life I would put $100.00 in church every Sunday evening.   But in my time of need I called for help.

He couldn't help me nor did he check on me as far as my situation, but will be the first one quoting me as his daughter doing service. I could go on and on, but again the only thing that remains the same is a tree. Never put your trust in "man", trust only GOD.

I have met some really good pastors and overall it's up to me to save my soul and get closer to my Creator and accept Jesus in my life. On the strength of being openly gay it's a lot of open debating about that, but at the end of the day only one person has the right to judge me on Judgment Day. I really feel like so many pastors are straight-up pimping pastors.   Now that I am sitting behind the bars I have found myself reading quotes and enjoying the word on my own.   I am still able to plant seeds by helping other inmates that do not have anyone at all to encourage them or provide them with any of the things we are able to receive.   To simply give a bag of chips, a candy bar, or even order a extra fresh Friday favorite.   The grateful smile you see on a person's face is truly a blessing within itself.   It's time that my homosexual lifestyle is questioned as I get closer to my Creator, but judgment day will be the day he determines the overall love in my heart.

I opened up doors to a community that politicians have no clue about unless they are living in it or see it.   I have personally feed year after year an entire gay community doing gay pride events.   It wasn't one or two people that depended on me, but rather the entire community. I made phone calls to get help with HIV/AIDS testing.   I made the events fun so that people would come out to be tested.   My problem is why is it so easy for our politicians to meet about these issues and also put grant funding in the wrong people hands and think they have addressed the problem because it's solved on paper.   Honestly it is not! I solved a lot without assistance.   I took care of a community.   Politics are all about who you know and not necessary about those that care. President Obama spoke a lot on living certain experiences. Try getting involved in your community sometimes. The fact of the matter is AIDS and STD's are not going anywhere.

You just can't appoint anyone to take care of certain situations. I enjoyed it to the fullest, but my addiction led me to other bad situations. I now know my purpose. My journey is not over with as of yet!

I now wonder if the jurors used my homosexuality against me. I know no matter what, GOD still loves me. I never tried to hide my sexual preference. I made those who never understood really understand. I spoke to parents with children asking what if my child ends up gay and they can't accept it. I tell them first of all you must try to understand it. I can't honestly say I have all the correct answers, but I will talk from experience and be honest, comical, and give everyone a better view on the subject.

Society is so judgmental on other's sex, race, religious and all. I know that racism and judging others will always exist in this world, but once a person gets to know who they are deep inside and remember the first thing you pretty much learned in your ABC's, that "I" comes before "U" then most likely you are not going to care what others think of you. GOD has a job to do, just allow him to do it.

To be outnumbered by a group of people not trying and pressed for time in understanding your sexual preference. To be called names like dyke, soup cooler, faggots, hell bomber, etc is just what you have to face as people say for being different. What makes us as people so different than others? We are no different. We simply are still loving, smart, creative, outgoing and capable of making mistakes just like the next person.

So many people make it harder on those that have a strong mind to deal with the judgment of the people. What about the young man I talked out of wanting to kill himself over the Christian friends and family homosexual beliefs? Stop and live through Christ!

Chapter 3

The Following Day in Jail
June 16, 2014

All I could think about was getting up on Monday to call Tom Pace again! I wanted him to answer the phone and help me out. I didn't have a lot of time on my last calling card until new ones arrived, but I had to call back to Oklahoma City. I got up and prayed, exercised to strengthen my body and jumped in the shower. After I got out of the shower I called again. The jail recording announced "you have a prepaid call from an inmate in the Pulaski County Jail.

"Hello." A nice deep and well mannered voice answered.

I said. "Hello, may I speak with Mr. Tom Pace."

"This is Tom." He answered.

My heart started racing and tears formed in my eyes. My voice started to tremble uncontrollably.

"Hey, Mr. Pace, I read your book "Mentor: The Kid and The CEO. I wanted to write you but there was no address. So I called this

number that I found inside your book. My name is Angie Richardson. I am in Little Rock, Arkansas charged with aggravated robbery. Due to the fact that I did not know the law and was advised not to take a bench trial due to the judge on the case."

Tom asked. "Were you advised to take a jury trial."

"Well I wasn't, but I was not advised to take one as well, Sir, and was pretty much scared out of the bench trial. Listen, I am very well known here in Arkansas and a lot of people really look up to me. I really want to help some of these youngsters coming in here that has no clue in life. Some gang related looking for a family and making wrong decisions. There is one female in here that is only twenty-one years old and is charged with eight aggravated robberies. They have offered her thirty-three years in which she will have to do 70%. I do not want to see her life go like this, Sir." Tears rolled out my eyes.

"Well, Angela, you have to do the right thing by helping her." He said.

"I want to help the youth, Tom. Listen, my minutes are about to run out, but will you help me get my book published and give me an address?" I asked.

The jail house recording came on saying, "you have sixty-seconds."

"I will try, okay?" he replied.

"Thanks a lot and I will call again soon and write, okay Sir?

I wrote down the address with the thoughts of anything is possible through prayer, faith, and hope. When you finally make up your mind that you are ready to do something nothing will be able to stop you.   I believe and I receive through it all!

My pencil was so small that I could barely continue to write. The lead was so short and weaken.   My fingers were red from trying to and not wanting to stop writing.   The air was turned off in the units today and being closed up in a cell with Justice irritated me.   Her raising hell and wanting to smoke led me to read positive words and pray for my sanity to stay with me.   I'm so thankful that I am not a smoker.   My heart was weakening from missing so many people and overall not being able to be with Mrs. Washington in the last days of battling lung cancer.

She reminded me of my mother whom I lost to cancer in 2000.   I truly am thankful I was able to spend as much time with her and for the untouchable memories that I have of her.   I was in a serious relationship with her daughter, Keacia, years ago.   We are still like family.   This has been the most painful and the worst nightmare of my life.   I wonder if I hadn't been behind bars would I be so successful today.

I do know that GOD didn't sentence me to do all these years, but has lead me on a journey,   that I will soon Be able to call a vacation,   to allow me the opportunity to mentor and touch other's lives. Meanwhile, they will be touching my heart by sharing their stories as well.

As I set again on the hard iron steel writing in the heat in cell #221 a deputy appeared at the door with mail.

"Who is Angie Richardson, I have mail for you?" The deputy asked.

Hi Angie Bangie!

How are you doing girl?   I'm praying all is well with you.   I just wanted to write and let you know I love you, I'm thinking about you, and I am praying for you.   Never forget girl how strong you are and that you are a soldier. Never forget that you have a story to tell and with that big giving heart of yours and your comedy talent you can tell it from anywhere. Use that talent Angie and share the joy of laughter with the people around you now. You have a gift. Don't stop using it. Don't lose the faith, Angie. Trust the Lord. Know that GOD is bigger than everything. Know that HE is your shepherd. Know that you are blessed to have people that love you, family and friends. Unfortunately, I can't bust you out of that damn place, but I will try to make it more comfortable for you. I will put money on your books weekly. Angie you can count on that. I will write and encourage you and I will visit. I have minutes on my

phone so you can call me without using your calling cards or you can write me. Let me know if I can send you stationary or postage paid envelopes.

Keep your head up, Angie Bangie! Keep smiling and showing them two buck teeth...lol

I love you, Angie, and that ain't no bullshit!

Kim

Along with the letter I got quotes with words of encouragement and a very beautiful computer photocopy of the cover of my first book that I published titled *"Angie Richardson, I Have A Story To Tell"*. I took the photocopy out to show the other women. They all asked about copies of the book and how they could stay in touch. I inspired so many lives and I personally walked over to KT.

I said "look, come over here. You see this picture. I'm going to continue writing to reach out to others. I'm going to help you somehow, okay?"

She replied, "I really hope so, I need it."

I picked up the letter she wrote back to me after I reached out to her. KT is only twenty years old, 5'3", 122 lbs, nice pretty dreads, nice dark skin, and the cutest little smile and dimples. Something just drew me to her. I always make sure if I'm eating snacks to always share with her. I had no clue she didn't have anyone and her mother battled with drugs.

KT told me that she had been charged with eight aggravated robberies. I asked her what happened. She and her so called hood homeboy robbed plenty of gas stations. As they were running out the store she got shot in her hip. She now walks with a pretty bad limp. The prosecutors offered her thirty years in which she would have to serve 70%. She told me that it was no way she would tell on her friend that was with her, but when she got shot he ran away and left her for dead on the side of the building. The store clerk called 911 to get her some assistance. She admitted that they offered her less time if she would tell who was with her. There is no way she is going to snitch on her neighbor hood homeboy even though he left her to die and he is currently serving time on prison on other charges. I'm in deep thoughts after reading this letter from her. Am I a true mentor if asking her to come clean and have a life outside of these bars? What would you do?

KT's Letter

Thank you for your kind words, it is not too many that's going to do what you are doing. They are too focused on drama. I know this jail is child's play compared to prison. I did fall short, but I am going to get back on it because I have been through a lot and I have a lot to say that people can relate to. I have faith in my music. There is more to it than just money and cars. I wished I could have been more focused out there, but everything happens for reason. I know GOD has a plan for me. If I wasn't in here, most likely I would be dead with all the killing that's going on with my hood beefing with Monroe Street.

Every time I get on the phone or get a letter I hear about somebody I know getting killed. Since I have been here this has been an every week thing. I could have very well been in the mix of it all or at the wrong place at the wrong time. I am so ready to leave, but to Be real I don't think my mind is ready. You can feel yourself, but you can't feel GOD. He knows our heart and I think of it as he's keeping me here due to what the outcome could be if I get out. If I make bond I could dig a hole that I am in even deeper. So if he ever opens up the doors to let me go home before I have to do my time I will be happy, but if not I know it's for my own good. I have grown a lot since I have been here. I never really ever read the Bible and the last time I went to church is when my TeeTee stop making me go. Since I have been here I read the Bible every day. I have the one titled "Free On The Inside". I could never understand the Bible before, but the one I have now is very easy to understand. You asked me to make a list of what I wanted out of life. Seven months ago it would have been full of things that don't even matter now. I no longer want those things and would rather have peace, love, and a worry free life. Listening to other people talk about how it was when they were growing up shows that my age group is going to end. It's coming soon. I want to better myself to prepare me for it. Someone is helping me change my life and I want to help change someone's too. I want my music to open up people eyes, ears, and hearts.

KT

Chapter 4

Discovering My Purpose in Life

I made sure I listened to KT's rap lyrics. She is very talented with her lyrics through her life's experiences at such a young age. I made sure to pray for her and asked her to pray at all times no matter what storms she has faced. It bothers me to see her walk around without any help from the outside world, but everyone is not fortunate to have that type of love and support. It's important to know how blessed you really are doing a time of needing people you think love you. I try not to be a bother to anyone because they know we need some type of help. GOD has made away and you have to believe it to receive it. I did know for sure that KT and I were both going to Newport, Arkansas prison for women. I knew that plenty of women were going to try us. My goal is to try and get her and others that I knew respected me to get their spiritual minds and thoughts together. To stay out of trouble, enroll in positive classes and programs offered and to pray for healing of their minds and spirits. To pray away all the evil spirits

that really exists inside and outside this world. I asked her to kindly talk to her public defender and ask her to get the prosecutors and DA to come down on the thirty years with the 70% mandatory. I know that I didn't understand a lot about my case and was unfairly sentenced.

I feel as if the State should somehow reconsider certain sentencing guidelines and situations. I know people that have committed murder and are walking the streets. I know that different programs and mentors can impact someone such as KT's life at the young age of twenty. She deserves punishment, but 70% of thirty-three years? Most likely she will be institutionalized if her mind isn't focused. She will get released and commit another crime or hopefully finds someone that wants to help her. Even in the midst of trying to get my own sentence reduced I still have my mind set on helping the LGBT youth. I see too many getting into trouble. I do not want them to think it is cool to see me in this same uniform. It's not at all. I highly regret it. I'm going to show so many here there are so many other things in the world to enjoy besides standing head count, a hard iron bunk, closed up in a cell all day, the worst food ever, not being able to talk on the phone whenever you want to, listening to all the arguments and screaming, sickly people, smelling different odors and most of all hearing "I need a flush." I knew that so many people talked about me in such a negative way, but those who actually got to know me love me just as much as I love them. No one could ever in this lifetime feel all that I've felt dealing with an entire LGBT & Diversity community and still be able to write and be successful while facing so many years behind bars. I didn't care about the article written up in the newspaper. The journalist has a job to do and so do I. He is doing it for the newspaper and I'm sharing my amazing purpose in life that GOD has given me and shown me favor with. I'm doing it for the Vine and GOD is the Vinedresser.

AngieSaidThat

One thing I can say is that everything I vision is done. GOD has revealed it all to me. The devil has stepped into my life and is mad over the fact I know this battle is not over for me. Right now as I sit on the iron hard stool I decided to continue writing. My butt was hurting so I placed my shower towel on top of it to relieve some of the pain, but these fingers were onto something that I am yet to see soon. My sentencing being reduced! I know GOD is going to stick to his promise and for me to stick to my new-found purpose behind the bars as a mentor and writer.

Did it take for me to get locked up to find my purpose in life? Is writing my purpose in life so that I may be guidance to others?

I can honestly say that my friend, Vona Cox, text me in May of 2014 and told me I needed to find my purpose in life. I really had no clue as to what she was talking about. She always text me such amazing words of encouragement that always made a difference in my day. I wish that we had text a lot more often before 12-12-12 versus after the nightmare, but she helped my mind. If it had not been for her I would not read the books that I read now or even take out the time to read. It's strange that I really enjoy writing, but hate to read. Now I really don't have a choice with as much time as I have. I want the two words, faith and hope, to make me feel like the thrill of night clubbing and a cold Bud light did. I finally found out David in the Bible wrote "The Lord is my Shepherd" while protecting his sheep.

The fact of knowing I would return again and put my enemies to shame with all my mentor movements and books was comforting. I claim it in the name of Jesus. I believe it. I receive it. I will not do the time that was unfairly sentenced to me. I am worth so much more to any state outside of the bars versus being behind the bars. I will be able to help our youth stay away from trouble and make better decisions in a time of trouble instead of not having all the facts. I care. It is not just a job to me. It replays repeatedly in my mind how my public defender said to me.

"I'm going to "get paid regardless", I work for this judge and I wouldn't do a bench trial."

To get punishment is one thing, but to be ineffectively advised is totally different. To know that KT has eight aggravated robberies pending, was actually caught with a gun on the property and we almost got the same amount of time! I'm thinking everyday that my sentence reduction is worth fighting for and by all means I am going to do it too! So many people sit around this jail and complain, but don't take any steps trying to get a turn around on the court's or jury's decision on their life.

I ordered phone cards, pencils, writing pads, and postage stamps to conquer my destiny. I make sure that it is not always about me and care for others. For those who want to get the answers I am willing to team up with them And join together for change, but there are those that enjoy the respect of jail and prison life. Three meals and an iron bunk is living the life to several. There are also woman in this jail that really need to be admitted into the state hospital. To see these old women who are separated from the other inmates chained down like slaves walking through during the one hour that they have out simply weakens my heart. Most of these old women smell worse than the other inmates; they reek of urine and spread feces on the walls that actually stay on the walls for days. It has to be a better way. Surely if people are being punished for cruelty to animals, then why are we living in these conditions in jail?

Chapter 5

Another Day of the Long Journey

The devil has his way especially when he knows some people are weak, will easily sin, and have evil spirits. When I woke up today my mind was in such a great place. I got up shortly after standing head count, although I never got up for breakfast. The most pleasing thing for me to do was to continue dreaming about something I could no longer control…living outside of these bars. I had my mind set to go to the Law Library to research information on how appeals work. I wasn't going to give up the fight on the unfair sentencing and getting my time reduced. I also knew this battle was above my thinking level so I had to call on David, Joseph, Jesus, and GOD. Truly and surely if David protected the sheep I have a chance at getting my sentence reduced. I believe it. I receive it. But I fully realize I have to do more than just pray about it. I have to have faith, but I also must do the work. The Bible teaches that faith without works is dead. I needed someone who understood the law and how appeals work.

My cellmate, Justice, also signed up to go check on her case as well. Something she had going on with her food stamps (SNAP) benefits. I knew the deputy named Jerrie, who was working on the shift. She escorted those who Signed up to the Law Library. Some people have actually gotten out after obtaining an understanding of the law versus not knowing the rules of the justice system. Which I am one that didn't have a clue, but I did know my sentencing was unfair. I repeat again, I have no convictions, I never owned a gun and I was never seen with a gun. Marty, whom was already on probation for three gun charges and was openly seen on camera holding a gun, had his charges dropped for aggravated robbery to simple robbery and yet I get sentenced to damn near life. I was scared out of having a bench trial by my court appointed public defender.

We spent about an hour in the law library trying to find ways to make sense out of what really doesn't make any sense to anyone, not even the deputies. Because of the rules of their jobs the deputies can't speak on it or really be involved with the inmates. We are no longer human beings inside the jail. People tend to forget who we were to them on the other side of the fence.

While just sitting in my cell I decided to get up and exercise by doing yoga. What a great feeling it is to work out the mind and the body! I meditated and talked to GOD about this journey in my life. I also prayed for my cellmate, Justice, at a time in which she really needed a prayer warrior. She was screaming through the cell door at the guards and inmates. She cursed and complained about this and that, but the bottom line is we are all in jail. Do you really think these guards care about our complaints? It's just a job and some of the guards hated their jobs. Some did care from the heart, but very few.

The next day as I was walking downstairs I noticed the bottom level was filled with a bunch of people that were familiar with me and had many questions. They asked, "Are you the Angie that had the club?" Did you know I have liked you for years?" and "Did you know there was a big article about you in the newspaper?" I heard some of the other studs calling my name to ask if I was okay and saying to keep my head up. They also shouted out "they did you wrong!"

I walked back up to the cell and wrote letters to some of the young studs I knew in here.

Listen, we have to be positive in here. We as a part of LGBT community are already judged for our lifestyles so let's make sure we pray, drink plenty of water, and exercise our bodies, and be careful of our actions. I feel because of who I am in the community I must stay on you guys in here. I warned them that these females in here will play games with them, but to please handle it with a long handled spoon.

Much love and respect, AngieSaidThat

I looked out the cell's small window and noticed an inmate asking me to show her my six pack. Hell I don't even have a six pack. My mind wasn't even on any jailhouse homosexual activities. Ugh! I didn't know whether to be flattered or just pretend to be dead. I knew the younger studs would love the back and forth drama and attention from these women. I knew some inmates took their relationships seriously, while for most it was just something to do while incarcerated. I just simply was not interested. Even if I didn't have a special woman in my life, my mind was on nothing but my new found purpose in life and getting my sentence reduced. Period. I have faith and hope in getting the hell out of here. 3201 West Roosevelt, better known as the county jail, had to be the worst living conditions to hold anyone in, period. The unhealthiest environment even for the employees that clock-in daily. To witness some of the things I have seen in such a short period of time is shameful. I'm thankful I have been blessed with my writing skills and the ability to raise awareness of these awful conditions to the politicians of Arkansas. Not all politicians will care, but I trust GOD that some will have a caring heart. It could be someone they love locked up one day. HELP!

But speaking of the employees, a deputy noticed me standing in line. Our eyes instantly connected.

"What a player doing in here?" she asked.

I shook my head as she came from behind the desk to walk with me back upstairs to my cell. I looked at her and answered, "They have sentenced me as if I have killed the president, but I am going to fight it all the way to the Supreme Court if necessary." I also told her, "It's not fair and somebody will listen. I know that I am going to Newport, but not for twelve years, and I have faith if nothing else." Then I asked, "What's wrong with your head? I am not use to seeing you wearing hats."

We both laughed as she told me, "I'm getting it fixed tomorrow." She then stated, "Well I'm going back to my unit; you have too many eyes on you in here. I will be back to see you, okay?"

"Okay, do that for me", I smiled and said. I haven't seen her again, but I know if I was on the outside of these walls the conversation would be something like "You miss me? Or "Do you have a lady friend? People look at you totally different whenever the rabbit has the gun, and we all know it ain't no fun when the rabbit has the gun. I comfort myself by knowing that all the people that formed against me and had so much negativity to say, do not know what a strong minded person of faith and hope that I am. And no weapons formed against me shall prosper. I am sitting behind bars facing twenty-one years in prison and GOD has delivered me and made me successful with my writing pads And two small pencils that I can barely write with to be honest.

He has revealed to me to be careful with what I do with my hands, feet, eyes, and ears. I had more faith in my long term play dad and attorney friend than I had in my own Creator. It was no secret to the world and everyone knew how close our relationship had become over the years. But people told me I put way too much trust and faith in him. I too realized that after sitting here. Although I did not have $10,000.00 for him to represent me, he could have advised me on how a jury trial works. He could have told me that the people selected for jury duty have no expertise of the law. They didn't know anymore about the law than I did, but yet they would be the ones to sentence me. No one knows how much this hurts me. I love this little short white man more than I love my own father to be honest. To even vent about it causes tears to roll down my face. My spirit isn't going to allow him to sleep once I pray about it and release the disappointment and pain.

As the day went on coming back in our dusty blue uniforms from the law library watching the men in the hallways had me feeling some type of way smelling all the different odors. The vile odors made me think some of the men needed to order a douche from the commissary list. The musty hallways with the bad awful body odors were punishment enough within itself. Ugh! All I can hear is, "Angie, Angie, what's up? Hold it down and keep your head up." Returning from the law library in a great mood after talking to one of the stud deputies and a few others, my Cellmate and I got searched and headed upstairs. I noticed Justice had a attitude, again. Her favorite guard was on second shift, Ms. B.

"Hey, how was the law library?" she asked while unlocking cell #221.

Justice replied, "I had the worse time. I didn't find out anything today and the guard was so mean to me, but she helped Angie, that's her friend."

I spoke up and said, "Well I had a great time and she was helpful. Justice, you need to quit complaining every time things don't go your way."

She walked into the cell and flopped down on the bottom bunk as if she forgot that all we had were worn out thin mats on top of nothing but iron hard beds. Her butt was already flat as those early morning pancakes she looks forward to some mornings. What was she possibly thinking flopping down on the mat?

I continued talking, "look Justice, don't complain about who you think know me. I don't make complaints about your favorite guard who allows you to go out on clean up every time she's on duty and how you back in here bragging about this and that. We are not children. You are fifty years old."

She started screaming, "Angie, I don't want to hear it or talk about it. She was very mean to me, but she helped You. I don't want to talk to you, leave me alone now. I don't want to get locked up in the Ad Seg room." This is solitary confinement.

I told her, "Girl, we are already locked up, so let me tell you this, I am not your child and you can stop all that hollering. You ain't going to bust a grape in Welch's backyard while you claiming you don't want to end up on lock down. You should have spoken to the law library guard versus getting all upset and throwing my name in it as if I had control of how she felt. I'm locked up just like you are and I'm trying to understand why I got all this time and no weapon shall be formed against me, period! I'm rebuking it all in Jesus name."

I was so relieved when Ms. B. came and got her out of the cell for clean up. I needed the time to myself to get back what she tried to rob me of, my peace. Is that a crime? I didn't want anyone bothering me. I couldn't use the phone to hear my special lady's voice before lock down and worse of all, I started my cycle. Ugh! I couldn't explain my feelings other than the fact that I just needed to pray the negative feelings away from me.

I had gotten rid of a lot of the negativity before I was locked up. I only wanted to read words of encouragement, to write, and most of all to pray. I found myself writing to three or four other inmates some words of encouragement and also to remind them to drink plenty of water. The women actually got to the point of asking me to write them something to help ease their minds. I really enjoyed doing It for the ladies and to know that I was able to do it as I too was learning assured me that no matter where I was GOD could use me. The fact that the women enjoyed my letters and reading my thoughts also lets me know that GOD was with me every step of the way and I had found my purpose. I was expanding my mind and helping others by doing something I hated to do at home, simply reading. I crawled up in the top bunk to continue to write after everyone appeared to be asleep. Writing is my purpose even in the dark. A small light barely allowed me to see, but still I wrote. GOD did more in darkness until HE discovered light.

Chapter 6

The Lord Is My Shepherd

I placed my back against the hard brick wall. To my left was a small window with two bars. My cellmate returned about an hour later from clean-up. In that amount of time she had three disagreements with other inmates. She came in without saying too much of anything. I mean quiet as a church house mouse and it didn't bother me at all. I enjoyed the peace and I was able to concentrate on my writing. You have to conscientiously put your mind into the right place. All you hear is banging and voices from the male inmates upstairs in heated arguments and women inmates talking through the toilets and vents.

There really was no such thing as peace unless you truly found it within yourself.

I ended this day feeling good before going to sleep. My spirit had me in the right stage of mind. I knew the devil worked the day and night shift in this place. I was no longer a player on his team and he had it out for me. As I continued writing in the dark with very little light the mat on the iron bunk bed started hurting my butt. I freely expressed to these women it's so much easier to give up, but all we have to do is repent for our sins and within five seconds or less GOD has forgiven us and he still loves us. I had joined a new team that not even the State could compete against. Jesus died for my sins and GOD has Promised me something in return if I keep the faith and hope.

I knew without a doubt the devil was going to continue to appear, just as he did in my dreams saying, "Not guilty!" That dirty red bastard. Now look at the time I'm facing. He was highly pissed that I stopped shooting dice, that I changed my surroundings, and that I had found myself getting closer to my Creator and I knew he would try to find another way into my life. So what's next now that I am facing twenty-one years in prison and writing to reach out to share my story and the life stories of others. His face is even hotter. I have curly blond hair so he may as well consider me as one of the sheep that David protected. The Lord is my shepherd and I shall fear no evil! So you can back up from cell #221. I'm protected by the blood of Jesus in my dusty blue uniform, orange shoes, white socks and the gap in my teeth. AngieSaidThat So I decided to turn up the power, I just couldn't back down. I will continue to live by faith, hope, prayer and to thank GOD every day. I didn't care what the devil and the bunch had to say. I will not stop writing. The time didn't matter as far as my purpose is concerned, but it truly matters as far as my unfair sentencing. The State allowed twelve inexperienced people with no expertise of the law to decide my fate. I'm sure some probably hated gays, one looked drugged out and drifted off to sleep. I surely must put a mountain mover on them!

"Angie, wake up, Miss Sherry is leaving. She is being transferred to Newport." I assumed it had to be about 3:30 AM. I jumped up off the top bunk, walked to the locked cell door and waved goodbye.

"See you when you make it there", Sherry hollered.

Sherry is in her early fifties, has black and gray hair, and is somewhat over weight for her height. She was sweet and funny. She was facing a robbery charge for walking inside a credit union demanding money. She explained how she woke up with past due bills and had been on a crack spree for a few days. She told her daughter she planned to leave the house around 9:00 AM dressed as a man and was going to rob the credit union and would be back home by 9:30 AM. She entered as soon as they opened the door and placed a plant in the walk-way to keep the door open and a stick in the second door. She walked up to the teller and demanded the money. She went back home and gave some money to

her daughter to pay the past due bills and put up the remaining money. Meanwhile, a few days later she got a call from someone saying that she was on the news for stealing a ring off the finger of a woman that was having a seizure at the electric company. I asked her to tell me what happened. She started talking as she puffed on her cigarette.

"Angie, I was waiting to pay my light and this lady in line had a seizure and fell out. Girl, I noticed this nice diamond ring on her hand. So I bent down and started fanning her and slid the ring off her finger. Then I went and sat down as other people tried to help her. After the customer service rep. called my name I completed my Business and left. I sold the ring for almost $800.00. Just so happened her sister, who was a friend of mine, worked there also. They brought her another ring because I was not going to return it because I wanted to get high. The detectives took me in to question me and let me go. But a few days later I was turned in by a crack head from the neighborhood that had given me a ride from the credit union. The bitch was upset because I only gave her $10.00. I have been to prison eight times and now I'm back here to do 18 months." As she talked she smoked and wiped sweat off her face.

I looked at her and said, "You mean to tell me you have been in and out of prison eight times and have to only serve 18 months and I didn't even have a record, but they have given me all this time? Plus I have never owned a gun nor have I ever been seen with a gun. I don't understand." I said.

She said, "Yeah, you shouldn't have taken a jury trial. Those people don't know anything about the law and they are not your peers. They just got picked, Angie, to serve on the jury just to finish up the case as quickly as possible."

"I see now, but I didn't know plus I wasn't advised properly. I was just another case they wanted to close, but trust me, Sherry, I will continue to fight for the reduced sentencing that is due me and get out of here." I spoke clearly and with authority on this mess.

She explained how she didn't like talking about her case around the younger people because it is not okay to break the law even though she was battling a drug problem and owed the dope man money or her life.

I was able in such a short period of time to calm these women down when the guards didn't know how to talk to or treat them. They treated the inmates as if GOD had stopped loving us. People probably think this so only jailhouse talk and behind the bars struggle, but I am here to tell you the struggle is real inside and outside. Just because I am in this dusty blue uniform it doesn't make the president, judge, pastor, rapper, actor or anyone else no different in my Creator's eyes. These people have given me time as if I have killed someone. I am actually in here with murders that have less time than I do. For the record, I don't waste my time being worried about other's crime and time, however I do compare the unfairness of all.

Chapter 7

Faith & Hope

I finally talked to my good friend, Vona, after trying to contact her several times. I needed her address to write her and so that she could write me and send me words of encouragement to help me get through this storm until I could see the rainbow.

I remember a quote Oprah said during the queen Maya Angelou's home going. *"My faith is what I live on and will forever have no matter what I'm facing." It's my faith and hope that helps me to cope and survive daily."* I will be released in Jesus name, hopefully soon.

As I continued to write my spirits were high. I'm certain that inmates all over the world have issues and will try breaking the rules. Some of the guards also bring their personal issues to work with them. The only way for me to deal with this Pulaski County Jail @ 3201 W. Roosevelt time or even when I get to Newport is through my faith and hope. I'm not worried about anything other than preparing myself mentally, emotionally, and physically for this journey. I can't do it without my Creator standing with me.

This is truly an eye-opener of all the years that I have helped so many others and at a time when it counts the most I realize that people only really love you when they can possibly use you. Everybody loves a winner! Realizing This hurts and it makes me feel so bad. But when you get in tune with your spirit, when you feel what I feel just to pick up a pencil and express how wonderful it is to feel free even in the midst of facing twenty-one years in prison it is simply amazing!

Do you really know the meaning of peace, love, fearlessness and to be humble? You may want to Google it, but there is nothing like feeling it and living it!

Remember the very first time you tasted a delicious slice of cake that you really wanted? How just the taste of it made you feel inside? I remember that moment, but I never thought about all the ingredients it took to make that cake taste so good to me. All I knew is that I wanted another slice. Life on the outside is just like that.

My point is sometimes we forget about what it takes in order to make us feel a certain way. We often skip over the steps it takes, but are ready for the outcome. All these years I skimmed over so much in order to get to a place I've never been in my life. A place that no one had to tell me about. It does not affect us all in the same way.

This is my only way to cope with my situation. What works for me, may not work for you. I enjoy making people laugh and I enjoy writing. That's cake to me!

A lot of people need rehabilitation to cure certain addictions, I once needed a doctor to help heal my ankle. She told me I would never be able to walk straight again.

Since I have been here, I have put pressure on my ankle. After writing my book "Unfiltered" I stopped my gambling addiction. I have inquired about going to relapse classes. I want to learn more. The spirit of gambling is over in my life. The power of believe it and receive it is so true!

I noticed my eyebrows growing back as I walked outside to share the gift of laughter with the other inmates with my comedy talents. They all gathered around to listen to what I had to say. Both the State and Federal inmates know there are all kinds of programs in jail and prisons, but why not a monthly comedy show? It's nothing like laughter for the soul! I performed my comedy at hair shows, night clubs, private parties, and for patients in the hospital. Why not for those that are locked up? GOD isn't punishing me. He is actually healing me and using me to become powerful, successful, and to be the best writer in spite of my situation. The best movies come from a novel. This is real life and this is my story!

This is the most uncomfortable way to write. My butt, fingers, neck, and back are aching, but I'm not backing down. This is my purpose in life and I'm sticking to it, now just to get through it!

With the continuing growth of my eyebrows I found out that an inmate by the name of Kelly had a skill to keep them nice and neat. I noticed the great job she did on other inmates and asked if she would arch mine. She would take a piece of string hanging from the dusty uniforms and remove unwanted facial hair.

A pale little skinny white girl walked up to a table of black inmates and said,
"Someone needed Kelly, who is she?"

Another inmate said, "Kelly is a white girl."

I looked over to a table full of Mexicans and said, "Now go over there and ask who is NaNa?" We all laughed.

Yesterday's thoughts are tomorrow's hopes. I knew I would not always have days like this. I thought of all the funerals I would not be able to attend.   Your freedom has been taken, but there are a lot of people that aren't locked up and they don't feel free.

Saturday, June 21, 2014

Last night I had so much on my mind after making my last phone call to my good ride or die friend, Denise Parker.   She is so real that it's just amazing.   She opened my eyes up to an even more peaceful spirit. This peacefulness helped me to release something that brought tears to my eyes and thankfulness to my Creator at the same time.   I spoke about how I was represented by a public defender and about a great attorney friend of mine that has been in my life for years.   He was like a father figure and a great role model to me.   Truth be told, I still referred people to his firm and he has settled some great business matters for me. I talked briefly with Pookey and two other people that truly knew how I respected him.   They told me they saw him in court a few days ago and he expressed to them that there Was really nothing he could do for me and simply shrugged his shoulders.   Well, I didn't have $10,000.00 at the time and he knows very well that money never was an issue.   We all fall short.   It could happen to anyone.   It's not so much of the fact that he did not represent me, as it is that he did not advise me as to how a jury is selected.   What would it have cost him to advise me of the consequences I was facing with a jury trial versus a bench trial?   He knew damn well I had more faith in him than I did in GOD, which is probably why I am facing this amount of time.   I could have dealt with being sentenced to some time, but to get twenty-one years and to have never owned a gun?   But yet he says he loves me as if I was his very own. Well I can't tell!   But now I know that GOD is really walking with me   no matter if I don't have the knowledge as to how a jury trial works, if I am broke or rich, have an addiction or not, in a new home or not.   My Creator has the last say to it all!

GOD will move mountains and free me when he is ready.   My faith, hope and prayers will touch the heart of those that know I was sentenced unfairly.   It will touch the heart of those that know the jury were not my peers, it will touch the heart of those that know I received ineffective counsel. I did not know and I shouldn't be punished unfairly for not knowing. This is why I will continue to write to educate others on how important it is to read, to ask questions about anything you don't understand, to know who really loves you, and most importantly to know that GOD loves and to put your faith and trust in him rather than in man.

Someone that truly loves you would not want to see this happen to you and at the very least not tell you what You are up against facing a jury trial. This really hurt me and caused me to shed tears behind the bars. I had to write him and express my inner thoughts and feelings. I feel so much better and I still love this little short white man.

Chapter 8

Disagreements & Disappointments
Saturday, June 21, 2014

Today I got into my first disagreement with my cellmate, Justice. Every day I give her my trays and always share my commissary with her as well. She doesn't get to shop. I don't smoke, but I made sure she has cigarettes and pretty much anything else you can possibly have in here. Every Friday I ordered her the special dinner boxes too. Today I asked her politely for a piece of her honey bun. I was craving for something sweet. She had three of them because she sells her pills to the other inmates in order to get some of the things she needs in here. She calls it hustling the inmates. She told me no and refused to give me a piece of her honey bun. I really felt bad that she had no one on the outside to care enough about her to put money on her books or even write her. She acted as if I had asked her to co-sign for me a new car. She got loud and wretched over a piece of a damn honey bun!

"Look I'm not going to open my honey bun until tomorrow. I am going to eat the cake they just served us", she screamed as if I wasn't in the room. "Here take my cake, I don't want it right now, plus I hate the taste of it. I tried it last week", she continued.

"Look Justice, sweet heart, I've made sure you have whatever I have in here. I don't even smoke, but you get cigarettes on the strength of these women wanting to get close to me", I said remaining humble. "This is so petty. I got food but I don't have anything sweet. And you tripping over a damn honey bun? Let's get this straight now, first of all don't expect anything else from me. You can still have those dog chow trays due to the fact that I don't eat them, but I can't just sit it outside the cell knowing you want it. GOD would not want me to act like that. I will still read the Daily Word to you as well, because you need Jesus, but no more special favors out of me. My heart is too giving for you to be this selfish and unappreciative! Let's just leave it alone, okay? "Humble turned into a loud tumble!

She went on to say, "You are going to let me say what I have to say to you. Yeah, you help me, but I can hustle. I want to eat my cake and save my honey buns for later or hustle them off for cigarettes."

Lord, the devil almost stepped and showed out in cell# 221. All I could think about was the movie *"What's Love Got To Do With It"* and how Ike Turner did Tina "Anna Mae Bullock" for not eating the cake. At the thought of me giving her free cigarettes I realized she's really simply using and hustling me too!

I looked at her and said, "Justice, I am trying to stay humble with you playa. So let's just leave this alone, okay? Don't ask me for anything. I got me at the end of the day." The door opened and the guard asked, "Angie, you okay?"

"Am I okay?" I asked and stated, "you guys never hear my voice nor do I bother anyone." I told her exactly what happened.

The guard thanked me and told Justice to hush her mouth and leave it alone as she closed the cell door.

I couldn't believe how things are actually taken for granted until I witnessed how these women get into it over bread, cookies, chips, juice, cigarettes, and even these dog-chow trays. And now I am into it over a damn honey bun! I found myself laughing, but in deep thoughts over the ill deeds of others.

I jumped up on the top bunk and had to read the Bible to soothe my spirits. I had to pray for myself and her as well. I had to remain respectable and be forgiving to cope with the person I was really working on, which was myself! This was going to be a rollercoaster ride facing so much time and already experiencing how petty things can be behind the bars and I am not even in prison yet, just the Pulaski County Jail!

Chapter 9

The Honey Bun Saga Continues

After the guard shift change, two of the nicest guards were now on duty together, Ms. B. and Mrs. Norris, and of course Justice told them her version of everything that had happened although I thought we had left the situation alone. But before I knew it Ms. B. came to cell# 221 asking if there was a problem over Justice not wanting to open her honey bun.

My first thought was, now I just prayed about this and here we go again over a damn honey bun. Justice only had eleven more days in here and I am facing twenty-one years, but I wanted to take my towel and nicely place it in her mouth for even bothering Ms. B. about a damn honey bun issue. Really just so petty!

Ms. B. is simply beautiful. She's in her mid-twenties, nicely tanned and nicely built with thin lips. Now she was the perfect "honey bun". She listened to what I had to say and told me that she noticed how I tend to mind my own business. In which I do, I am toofocused on getting a miracle. Damn anything this jail has to offer outside of prayer and hope of getting out of here. Damn that honey bun!

Justice simply abused food. She ate my tray and hers. She wanted to get out on clean up to get extra food, plus she would eat up my snacks. I have never in my life seen a woman eat so much. Not even hungry, just greedy! I looked down at her toes and instantly thought about a reptile. Her toes were long and yellow and pointed at attention. Maybe this jail should also take fingerprints and DNA samples at intake processing for parasites before booking in some inmates and AngieSaidThat

I was so glad that Justice was once again out on clean up so that I could be in the cell alone to write. During the few hours we had out, the first thing I did was call my baby to check on her. I made sure I called her every day. If I didn't call she already knew I wasn't out and able to. I called just in time. She was at my twin niece's birthday party, Bailey and Madison. She put them on the phone and my heart dropped as tears started rolling from my eyes. I had to drink some water to keep my voice from trembling.

Madison spoke clearly, "Aunt Angie, why are you not at our birthday party?, she asked.

I lied, "Baby I am out of town, but I am going to make it up to you. I love you and enjoy yourself, okay?"

"Okay, I'm going to put Bailey on the phone."

"Hey, Aunt Angie, I want to see you", she said softly.

I said, "Look baby I am out of town, but I love you, okay?".

My niece said, "I love you, too" as my heart wept.

I talked to Boss Lady for a few minutes and told her to enjoy herself and we ended the call. I called a few more people and then went outside to talk to the other ladies that were smoking cigarettes. I could feel this one particular woman watching me.

She finally said, "Come here." I got up from the hard concrete I was sitting on and walked over to see what she wanted.

"Angie, you knew I wanted you in the free world and I am so disappointed in you, but I am also proud of you because it's almost as if you have a fan club in here. These women circle around you and you entertain them. You have them laughing and wanting you, but I don't want to see you getting mixed up in any of this. Plus these women are not on your level. I really respect you and why is it that you won't give me the time of day? I just don't understand. These young studs in here really look up to you", Mamie said looking all serious and like Cupid just shot an arrow in her heart, Ugh!

I said, "Look, let me say this to you and I am being honest. As far as these young studs are concerned they are making the best of a bad situation. I speak knowledge to Them because I know how they look up to me, but you need to know I am human. I'm in the same dusty blue uniform as everyone else. You are judging me and that's not cool. I am not in here looking for or wanting to be with anyone. I have someone. I wasn't trying to be with you all these years when we were on the outside of these bars so why would I want to be with you now? The only thing I am focused on is my time being reduced.

These young studs are trying to have fun, so if they want to play with these women and these women allow it, that's none of my business. I talk to them about staying out of trouble and the power of prayer to change their lives. I am not concerned about anyone's relationship inside or outside these walls. I already know there's no such thing as a perfect relationship and I never promised anyone it would be easy for anybody."

She looked at me and said, "I really do like you and you are a very positive person. I really want to…"

I stopped her and said, "Look, I don't want you to be on suicide watch trying to be with me, Doll Baby, cause it ain't gonna happen!" We both laughed out loud as I walked off thinking, "Girl Boo…NOT!

During the next hour that we were allowed out of our cells I suggested we play a game called "Dirty Hearts". I dealt the cards to those who wanted to play and if you were dealt a heart someone could ask you any question they wanted to and you had to answer honestly. Many of the inmates gathered around eager to play and some simply just To be nosey. Everybody was watching and listening. I was able to get the blacks, whites, and Mexicans to come together to laugh and have fun, even some of the deputies came over to listen to what questions were being asked and answered. My nights had gone from throwing events and clubbing to entertaining the inmates behind the bars. I really had all the women cracking up and laughing. To be able to provide some enjoyment to these women was amazing! And the fact that I was sitting around a gated wall next to murders, child abusers, an educated school teacher with two masters degrees and an arsonist who burned seven buildings confessing to crushing and wanting me, tickled me. Why is it always about sex? I treated them the same as I would any other woman outside of these bars, not interested. Since I have been here in this short amount of time I realized that if I am in favor of working on myself and getting closer to my Creator then I am not the one to judge anybody. Tonight was actually priceless and overall I am thankful that my spirit has the best of me and has been lifted.

I went back to cell# 221 after the dirty heart game. Our last hour was so hyped up with excitement that I didn't get to take my shower, so I washed up in the sink inside the cell.   I snacked on some tuna from commissary.   With a clear understanding that this is a jail full of Mexicans and they taught me how to say lesbian in Spanish.

"Lesbiana" was my new jailhouse name.   I looked over and noticed one of the inmates from one of the downstairs units standing at my cell door. Her name was Toe-Toe.   She was in jail on Federal charges and had explained to me earlier that she had Given birth while doing prison time. I walked to the door to see what she wanted.

"Angie, downstairs wants you to come out with us and play the dirty hearts game.   We heard you got it started and it was fun", Toe-Toe said smiling.   "The ladies on the bottom floor want you to play with us too" she continued trying to get me to come back out.

I laughed and said, "No, I am about to write in my book."   I explained the rules of the game to her and told them to go ahead and play without me and to be sure and come back and tell me all about it.

"Okay" she said, "but you know it's not going to be the same or as much fun without you", she said as she walked back downstairs.

Chapter 10

Jailhouse Treatment & Secrets

I jumped back on the top bunk and continued to write about my daily life behind the bars.   The thought of how so many people got attached to me in such a short period of time was comforting.   It hasn't even been a full month since I arrived here but my amazing creative mind was on the rise with powerful prayers, my writing movements, and fulfilling my purpose in life.

The feeling I got at the thought and vision of so many people reading my story can't easily be explained other than to say I am blessed. Knowing all the materialistic possessions I once owned were now gone was okay with me because I know in the future I will be blessed as well as a blessing to others with a simple pencil and writing pad.   I didn't even allow certain things to bother me as far as people not writing or sending money.   I had a few family members and friends that believed in my vision.   They knew my power wasn't going to be easily taken from me anymore.   Once I picked up the pencil it was with ease and as if a peaceful spirit guided my hand to write the stories from behind these walls.

I didn't care about being on clean-up every day or stressed out about having time outside as the smokers did. The things I cared about were commissary, money orders, shower items, and having a clear and prayed up mind. Hope was the key to unlock the gates of Newport Prison once my appeal made it to the Supreme Court of Appeals. I felt really good about it. I didn't listen to my long term attorney friend, Stanley who said, "Oh, there's nothing I could do because you took a jury trial." This is not the end of it as long as I have the strength to write, the ability to reach out to others on the outside and a proper mind to pray. My Creator will touch someone's heart to help me to get my sentenced reduced.

Psalm 94: Arise O Judge of the earth. Sentence the proud to the penalties they deserve.

Again, this is a first conviction and I never owned or was ever seen with a gun. How long will the wicked be allowed to gloat? I have loosened those bad habits and let it go. To even get hostile was not in my character. I prayed and remained humble. I want to impress my Creator. Most probably think it's just jailhouse talk, but the heart speaks only for itself. This is truly a life transition. It's about me making a decision. I looked over at Justice and handed her a cigarette and gave her my tray. I am not a smoker, but some come to this jail and will cry out about a damn cigarette. To listen to another inmate speak about how badly she want a smoke is saddening. One inmate watched a deputy finish smoking a cigarette and licked the filter before throwing it to the ground.

"I bet you won't smoke the rest of this cigarette." Said the guard.

A lot of the mistreatment behind these bars wasn't even necessary, but truly the inmate picked up the cigarette and smoked it.

Some of these guards' problems were just as serious as the inmates. There is no need just to want to mistreat a person because of the uniform status. It could very well be your mother, father, sister or brother in the very same dusty blue uniform. Trust me! You never know how things could turn around. I once owned a nightclub. "Equality"

Through it all I found myself talking back to Justice. I even teased her about us getting into it over a honey bun which eventually got her moved out of cell# 221 in order for us to get along with one another. I understand her eating habits became even worse. It could've been a form of depression. I wasn't sure, but the relief from all the negativity was a blessed good feeling.

I also realized that a lot of the inmates bullied those who they knew weren't going to say much about it. It really didn't scare me about the charges or time certain inmates faced. My name alone had respect written all over it. I enjoyed more fun, laughter, love and caring, but anytime there are a lot of women in the same place at one time and on their cycles at the same time you can just imagine the drama. Many of the women enjoyed the laughter I brought, So I wasn't really having any issues, but some of these inmates are slicker than fish grease.

These women in jail have taught me a lot in this short period of time. I witnessed them fish through the toilets to the men upstairs to receive lighters, letters, and cigarettes. I tripped out watching an inmate continuing to flush the toilet until the spoon and the fabric connected. For whatever item you are trying to get to the male inmate upstairs the string and spoon have to connect to give the signal to send the item. Well, I'm sure now that I have exposed the jailhouse secrets the rules are subject to change. Will the improper mistreatment change as well?

Some things I couldn't get out of my head or get use to for that matter. As I sat close to the window in cell# 221 I could hear the rain pouring down hard and the thunder gave me chills. I prayed for the rain to bring a blessing inside the jail @ 3201 W. Roosevelt for a facility and an inmate treatment upgrade change.

Chapter 11

Death behind the Bars

Today was just the beginning of one of the most unexpected and too soon experiences on this journey. The inmate in cell# 215 died. I was awakened by screaming and the sounds of people running past the cell door. I sat up wondering what could possibly be going on? I looked out the door and saw a number of deputies and nurses in the back area.

I heard the inmate in cell# 222 screaming, "She's dead. I can feel her spirit. Please pray for her family." She instantly started praying. I closed my eyes for a moment of silence, but I could hear the inmate in the cell next door praying and reading her Bible at the same time. My inner thoughts were directing me to remain quiet and humble as surely my prayers would work in my favor.

I noticed the deputies and a medical assistant trying to find a power outlet. I assumed it was for some type of device to assist the inmate in cell# 215. She had only been in this jail for a little over two weeks. She wasn't able to push the button in her cell to call the unit officer on duty that night because the intercom system wasn't working in unit "C". She was found later by Sgt. Gib on the first shift not responsive or breathing.

She would cry out in the late night and early morning hours complaining that her stomach was hurting and she had severe pains. She continued to cry behind these bars, but who really cares if you are not in the authorized proper blue uniform? Yes it is true that the inmates uniforms are dusty and worn out, and have even been worn by other inmates and the deputies uniforms are starched, crispy clean, and mostly neat, but do we as inmates deserve to die over the difference? The inmates are still people we are humans too!   My GOD, I need you now!

Fact:
        If the proper rounds had been made and CPR was performed immediately instead of waiting at least twenty minutes for the officer on the next shift to do the standing head count the inmates life might have been saved.   Sgt. Gib had to have noticed the inmate in cell# 215 not standing or responsive as he looked in her cell yelling, "Standing head count, hey get up."   She didn't move.

He unlocked the cell door and walked in and lightly tapped her. No response.   He moved her arm and noticed blood foaming from her mouth. He checked her pulse. Again, no response. He called out over his radio, "Code Red", and all the deputies, sergeants, and medical assistants rushed to unit "C".

They screamed at the other inmates as we continued to watch what was happening, "Get out of the damn doors and on your bunks or you will miss your activity time and be locked down all day, damn it!"

I jumped back on my upper bunk and prayed. I found myself writing and at the same time thinking it could have been me or any of the other inmates. I am fully aware that there are inmates that will use fake illnesses and make it harder on the inmates that are in dire need of medical assistance, but should the truly sick be punished and have to die because of others behaviors? Is it that 3201 W. Roosevelt will cover up the raw truth to avoid law suits? Who would believe the criminal mind in the dusty blue uniforms over the crispy clean officer uniform? GOD will and he will have his way on judgment day!

I realized after that day the other inmates were also feeling some type of way. We later went outside to talk about the cries out for help and the death of the inmate in cell# 215. I wondered would it cost me even more punishment after what I have witnessed and experienced so soon in this jail, or will the Angels from above sent from the Man above with the higher powers to improve these jailhouse conditions.

My heart hurts to even write about the raw truth of it all. My mind constantly tells me that my faith and the truth will be my way to freedom from it all. I'm not listening to my attorney friend, Stanley, the inmates, the deputies, or the talk outside of these bars. My mind is made up to continue to my new found liberation and purpose of writing books. I will continue to read daily quotes to strengthen my mind and for wisdom.

Psalm 91:14-16
The Lord says:

"I will rescue those who love me. I will protect those who trust in my name. When they call on me I will answer. I will be with them in trouble. I will rescue them and honor them. I will satisfy them with long life and give them my salvation."

My body felt energized as I read my daily scriptures and filled myself with the words of my Father. My mind felt open and my heart was beating rapid with a true sense of hope. I have never denied my multi-talents, but behind these bars I am able to focus much better. There are correction officers, public defenders, and even my attorney friend, Steven, that have shown me that I do have feelings, but I also know that "The Lord Is My Shepherd".

I'm a writing fool! I've gathered more pencils, paper, and envelopes to take steps toward tasting that delicious slice of cake that I crave for on the regular, but this time I will know all the correct ingredients. I will appreciate it in the midst of baking it and I will serve others a piece of my creation. I may not be literally in a kitchen, but it's still tasty to be able to write about an amazing life experience as I continue to uplift other inmate's spirits and even praying over certain officers that have forgotten that we are humans, too.

Chapter 12

A Deputy's Life

*I*s it really just a paying job with benefits to most? To walk around after a death and make comments like, "Get over it, you are in jail." Wow! True enough and I fully understand that as sure as you are born you must die and I know that GOD will call you home at any time. I respect this to the fullest. My problem is my Creator has also blessed us to with medical assistance of all kind. What would it have hurt to simply get the inmate in cell# 215 to a hospital? Is it cheaper for us to just die?

However, not being able to call a family member or a love one and notify them of one's condition is when you realize that certain staff members really do have hearts. They are the ones who bluntly speak on situations and sincerely care. We all know that no one lives a perfect life, not even the people in the crispy blue uniforms. Some even end up wearing the same dusty blues that we are wearing. Then we have those that just didn't get caught. Some people need to be careful how they treat others. You should treat people the way you want to be treated.

Don't talk about other people's children because you never know what your own child is doing behind your back.

I fondly remember my close comedian friend, Superstar Jones. He was a police officer for over twenty-five years. He and I performed in a comedy show with one of the funniest and well known celebrity comedian named Eddie Griffin at the Robinson Auditorium. A few weeks after the show word spread like wildfire about the officer's alleged involvement in transporting drugs through the city. Instantly, I got on Face book to respond as people tried to belittle his character.

Superstar has always been a great father and family man. He served and protected our community with love and laughter. Even now as he serves time in Federal Prison I still love and respect him just the same. We continued to stay in contact throughout his ordeal and the love will remain forever. It doesn't stop with him. I can very well go on and on as far as the switch-out of the dusty blue uniforms and even about those that currently hold high power positions. I know that my addiction to gambling caused many to make jokes and laugh at me and I also know that if I had $10,000.00 I would not have gotten this type of time. Money is the root of all evil. Does this make Superstar or me a harden criminal?

Shortly after returning to cell# 221 I noticed a new cellmate. A much older woman. She looked as if her eye was swollen, slim build, red hair matted to her head that reminded me of a SOS pad. She also wore a pair of red prescription glasses. She had a mothball odor about her. She looked up from the bottom bunk and the first thing she said softly was,

"You need to get AngieSaidThat copy written."

I looked at her and replied back,

"Ma'am, how do you know my name?" I smiled showing my gaped teeth off as if I was doing a close-up commercial.

"Baby, it's written all over the wall and I figured it's your name and somebody might come in this cell and try to use it, you know?" She didn't smile and gave me a serious look.

"Ma'am, if you don't mind me asking why are you in here? I am writing a book and I would like to share the stories of certain inmates as well as my own story." I told her.

"Well baby, that's good, but don't put my real name in your book." We both laughed.

"No, I wouldn't dare do that." I grinned and said.

"I was riding down Pike Avenue to put one in me. I went to buy a gram of crack and was on my way home on Camp Robinson when a police officer got behind me. I kept driving because I was only a few blocks from home. I pulled up in the driveway and they surrounded my car." She explained.

"Mrs. Thomas why didn't you throw it out the window or swallow it?" I asked.

"Baby, I put it in my purse and couldn't find it, but it was some "fye." I mean some good dope. They had the police dog with them and it sniffed right up on it and here I am. I was trying to get a hit." She said.

I laughed, "Yeah, hit with a woof-woof by that police dog." We both laughed. "Are you married or do you have children?", I also asked.
"Yes, I have been married for forty-two years. My husband is retired military and has Alzheimer's. He's is eighty-nine years old and in a nursing home. We are both disabled military and we have one son." She continued to talk softly.

"So you must get pretty good money? What made you start using crack and does your husband know about your habit or did he know before his memory went bad?" I asked.

"Yes, he was aware of it. I always felt like I could control it over the years. I never did it in front of him. I really do need to stop." She explained.

"Well, I battled with a gambling addiction that controlled my everything. The devil knows his way to our weaknesses you know? Loving an addiction over good people or over GOD isn't good for you either, you know? GOD is a jealous man. The way you wanted that hit of Crack, I needed to hit the crap table with a seven or eleven on my first roll which meant I was a winner. But we are losers to allow any spirit of addiction to take us out of our character, Mrs. Thomas. Here is my Bible, you can read scriptures if you want to, okay?" I said and smiled.

"Thank you and I am going to buy a copy of your book. When is dinner served?" she asked.

"In about an hour. It's not the food of choice, but if nothing else eat your bread. I have plenty of commissary if you want a few snacks." I replied.

She continued to talk about how she hated that she went out for a "hit" and about how they impounded her car. I assured her it was because it was drug related. I looked down at her from the upper bunk as she was making sounds that sounded like a video game and farting at the same time.

Mrs. Thomas finally dosed off to sleep. She snored and had different noises coming from her body along with the farts and the smell of a teaspoon measurement of moth balls. I thought this is how we do it at 3201 W. Roosevelt. After all we are not at a hotel. As she peacefully snoozed, I asked "Why me GOD?" I used the thermal pants that Sherry left behind to make me a comfortable cushion under my butt so I could write. The good thing was she wasn't going to talk my ear off.

I knew that most of the inmates that were on drugs slept a lot after they were booked in. It was as if they forgot About life and thought about nothing but getting high and how the feelings of being high made them feel. I felt the same way over a damn square pair of dice, so I surely wasn't the one to judge anybody. I got close to the window in cell# 221 and read scriptures, prayed, and wondered what would the next day bring. I also found myself writing until I fell asleep.

Before I could get comfortable the guard in Unit C screamed, "Standing head count." Mrs. White, who was short, wore weave in her hair, and dark skinned had a serious look on her face. Mrs. Thomas was in a deep sleep and snoring like all three of the little bears, Papa, Mama, and baby bear. The snores got even louder.

I whispered to her, "Mrs. Thomas wake up, it's standing head count and you must be awake during the count to make sure you are alive. An inmate recently passed so trust me they are on this real tough."

Baby, when I tell you she popped up like a hot pop tart looking lost and acting as if she had forgotten she was at 3201 w. Roosevelt. She screamed, "I got to go to Wal-mart, I need a ride to Wal-mart!"

I looked over at her laughing and said, "Baby this is not the everyday friendly neighborhood store." I guess that hit of crack had her tripping and thinking she was going shopping at the neighborhood store. I said, "Mrs. Thomas, go to bed honey!" We both laughed and went back to bed.

I could not stomach the fact the tissue she had blown her nose with was laying all over the cell floor. I realized she needed to sleep her high off and I decided to address this tissue situation later when she woke up.

Chapter 13

Dear GOD

The following morning during standing head count Sgt. Gib was back as if he had never clocked out. His voice alone gave me irritating chills. "I need everybody standing, nothing on the tables, nothing in your windows, have your ID badges ready where I am able to see them. If you are not standing you will not get your activity time", he screamed.

Ugh! My first early morning thought. I closed my eyes and prayed in Jesus name. I prayed to my Creator for favor on a turnaround in sentence of this hurricane verdict. There wasn't anything for me to do but hold on to my faith and be patient with Him as he placed it all in order.

Sgt.   Gib is about 5'7", 160 lbs, glasses, and thin hair on the top of his head with a perfect part in the center.   He also had two little rotten teeth in the front that pretty much reminded me of raisins.   He obviously enjoyed having some authority.   He made sure we all knew he was the little small man with the power in Unit C.   Who needed a flush was him, a hush flush!   I was simply too sick of his mouth.

And what really made me feel some type of way about him is when he told Justice that the inmates needed to respect the people in authority and be the best slaves or prisoners that they could be.

About thirty minutes later we were allowed outside or to do whatever you decided to do on the morning activity time, rather it's a smoke, make phone calls, or shower.   We only got out of our cells two hours a day and some days not even that.   I was already sick of 3201 W. Roosevelt.

A few of the women came outside telling me that Sgt. Gib was in my cell doing a strip search.   I looked at them and said, "Yeah, right!" as I walked back in and up to the desk.   He said, "You had an empty Vaseline jar in your room with cigarettes in it and your name badge was hanging in the door window.   You need to wear it every time you come out of your cell.   I could lock you down for two hours."   He looked at me talking very seriously as he stood up and walked from the behind the desk.

I looked at him and placed my hand on his shoulder.   I knew from the look on his face that this was the wrong move towards this authorized blue uniform.   The expression on his face read, bitch please with two snaps and a circle! I quickly removed my hand and said, "Sgt. Gib, I have no rule that says your badge has to be on at all times when out of the cell.   Where are my cigarettes?   I give them to people that are in here without and need a smoke versus them having to pick up filters off the ground."   I smiled flashing my two buck teeth and gap.

"Well let me give you the rules that you should have received in orientation."   He said and smiled as he handed me a piece of paper.

I thought to myself how he just found a forty-eight year old middle-aged lady dead and now he is all up in my face and searching my cell and he's complaining about an empty Vaseline container and fussing at other inmates about weave hair. What he didn't know is that these women were not going to play games with him about their Brazilian hair, Boo-Boo. He obviously did not know that was going to cause a "Code Blue, Officer in need of back-up. Crispy blue uniform down over hair weave!"

To be locking a person down over a spoon, a fork, or an empty container was the proper rule or you could have your two hours of activity time taken, but what is the punishment behind the bars for allowing an inmate to cry out in pain for help only to be left to die? So, what are we to do in a situation like this?

Dear GOD,

I'm currently sitting @ 3201 W. Roosevelt facing time for aggravated robbery in which I never owned a gun. I was scared out of a bench trial due to the judge of the court. Is it just punishment because I never studied the law nor did I have a jury selected of my peers. I also feel my homosexual lifestyle and the fact that I am well known in such a closed minded community all played a part in it before even going to court. True enough I was acquitted in 2002, but those people were eventually caught. I never claimed to be perfect, but I claim Equality. This jail is not suitable for pets to be locked in. The vents are covered with thick dust and mold and mice running under the cell doors.

I know that Jesus got arrested as well as Timothy and Joseph. Lord, you all give me hope. I continually pray for the other inmates here on Roosevelt Road. GOD, did you all ever need a flush? I've sent a prayer request in your name Jesus to move mountains on the upgrades on the outdated 2006 handbook rules, plus July 8, 2014 honey buns that were delivered to us from commissary for full price and should have been on clearance. They were stale and outdated.

GOD, please show them that you are the one with the power and will turn this unjust sentence around.

Father, I love you,
Your Child
AngieSaidThat

Chapter 14

Visitation Hour

Visitations. We were only allowed one thirty minute visit per week. Depending upon your last name is how your visitation day is chosen. My visitation day fell on Tuesday or Sunday. You are allowed at least fifteen people on your visiting list. Three people are allowed to visit and must all come at the same time. There is a thirty day waiting period to add someone to your list.

My VP Boss Lady came to see me every Sunday. Sometimes Kim and my buddy, Yvette, came to visit. I enjoyed each and every visit with plenty of love and laughter. I also got special one hour visits from out of state visitors. I'm thankful to have those that took out the time to visit and laugh with me. It really helped my spirits. If something was bothering me I never let it show in front of them.

My buddy "Y" had done twelve years in Newport, Arkansas years ago.   She's the type of person that has a heart that's good as gold. I love her wholeheartedly.

Kim and I have been friends for many years.   She continues to do as she promised.   Genuine love and support through it all.

My Wife is just one of those Michelle Obama type of women. Simply sweet, caring, very appreciative and accepts my good and bad. It's hard to find women of her caliber these days.   People say it's a sin to love the same sex and that GOD will punish us.   Well, GOD also knows your heart and if it's so wrong to love like this then please allow Him to judge me.   She is my rock, but He is my everything.

I also look forward to the move to Newport because I hear you are not talking through a glass wall.   You are allowed to have contact visits for four hours at a time once a week.   It will surely make us both feel better on this journey until I get that final okay that I am free.

Until then I will continue to do as I have been doing, staying out of trouble, getting no write-ups, being a mentor, focusing on living my purpose and holding on to my faith.

The visitation booths are never cleaned on the inmate side or even wiped down.   I can only imagine the germs that come in and out of these small closed in rooms, but my heart aches the minute my lady walks away until our next Sunday visit.   During the moments when I am missing her like crazy I pick up a card she sent me and read it repeatedly.

"Love"

Being away from you is so hard.

I really miss your touch, just holding hands or feeling your arms around me, and oh your long slow kisses!   I really miss those.

I miss little things too. Like seeing your toothbrush next to mine, snuggling, joking or just being together in the same room.

The only thing that would be worse than this time apart from you would be not having you in my life at all.

Because I love who we are together. I love all the little things that make us "us."

My heart is with you. I just wish that the rest of me was too.

Your Wife

A visit by far that I was not expecting was from Brother Paul of Friendly Chapel Church. What a blessing! I was really surprised to see him and just as surprised that he even remembered me. After a very pleasant conversation he prayed with me and for me as we both placed our hands against the glass. I learned that day that you are still able to feel a special touch without being physically touched.

As I sat to continue writing and making corrections with my eraser a thought crossed my mind. I wished it was just as easy to erase 12-12-12. To make this correction would be the greatest turn-around of all times. Facing an amount of time that I truly didn't deserve, I quickly found a way to cope on a daily basis. I can't lie and say what the following day will be like for me in this prison life. I can say that I have truly been blessed with a gift. It has always been about unwrapping the box to see what's inside of it.

My gift contains something amazing that I am able to share with so many others. I can vision people reading the raw truth, real life stories at 3201 W. Roosevelt. I have been visited by people that I never thought would take the time to come and visit me, and I have also taken the time to allow others to taste a slice of my cake made with all the right ingredients to make it taste so tasteful. I am writing with my new-found liberal purpose.

I would take two small pencils and removed the sticky label from the Vaseline, lotion, or deodorant containers and place both ends of the pencils together and slowly ease the sticky apart around the center of the two to make the pencils longer. I would then take the bottom part of the eraser and bite down on it with my two buck teeth, which formed a small hole as if one of 3201 W. Roosevelt's mice had gotten a hold to it, and slide the eraser in the middle to secure the sticky tape. I had a much longer pencil to continue writing.

I will continue to write and serve the people my real life story as well as the stories and the cries of others behind the bars. If you need popcorn or the snack of your choice along with a drink, grab it and allow AngieSaidThat to entertain you with my writing skills until I am able to get a movie deal. Believe it, receive it in Jesus name! Allow the readers to say Amen.

Chapter 15

The Odors behind the Bars

I noticed an inmate in cell# 206 which is across the way from my cell watching me.   In my first two weeks behind the bars I received plenty of mail from other inmates.   Due to being well-known really plays a major part in my life.   They said to others I was the head leader of the LGBT Community.   The Lesbian, Bisexual, Gender & Transgender.

The stares from cell# 206 continued and from cell# 207.   After a while a note slid under the cell door and I opened it.

Hey, I think you are really cute.   I don't want you to think I'm crazy for watching you.   If you don't reply back it's okay, I understand. I just wanted you to know why I am always looking at you.

Cell# 206

I walked downstairs to go outside to walk laps around the small yard behind the gated bars. I wanted to think. I looked up after my second lap around and who did I see, cell# 207.

"Hey, you mind if I walk with you?" She asked.

"I'm cool, what's up?" I asked.

"My name is Monica, I have already heard who you are and about you. So, are you interested in a friend in here?" She bluntly asked.

"No, not interested, plus I'm in a relationship. I am not even thinking on the level." I replied.

"Well, I sure hate it. I really think you are cute." She smiled.

I knew my teeth weren't perfect, but she looked like she had dentures made of yellow corn pop cereal. I continued walking and thinking. Really! True enough I'm open about my lifestyle. I've made many historical movements in the LGBT Community. I couldn't stop thinking about how the prosecutor made me out to be a heartless monster. People that wanted to speak as my character witnesses were not chosen to testify that really could have told how I have blessed a community. True enough my sister, Sharon, spoke well and so did My Wife. However, I was told that others would be able to also. I was also told that if I talked about as far as what I do and about my LGBT lifestyle that could possibly get me even more time. The State was in such a rush with the trial.

Mrs. Copeland told me the truth about one thing. She was getting paid regardless. So deeply thinking, I told her that one of the jurors keep dosing off and she replied, "Oh, her arm is in the way and I can't see if she is asleep. Stop looking like you are mad, it could be used against you."

As I walked outside and continued thinking about it all, again the jury was not peers or people of my homosexual lifestyle. Do I really deserve twenty-one years and never owned a gun? In deep thoughts I walked twelve laps thinking;

Arkansas vs. Angela Richardson
Serving 12 years
Rebuke the devil, Rebuke this time.

I thought it has to be someone in the state of Arkansas that sees the unfairness of my sentence and ineffective counsel. Before I knew it I heard the officer say. "Lock down ladies." As I walked back up to cell# 221, Mrs. Thomas was pretty much out of her deep sleeping coma and she asked me if she could use my Irish Spring soap that I had ordered from commissary to wash her panties out. Ugh! I thought.

I assured her that I would get her some of the soap that the jail passed out, which is a small hotel size bar. All I could think about was the mothball odor, the video fart smell and the crust that must have been in the seat of those panties. She had them in her hand balled up like some homework. I'm sure there was enough crust in the middle of those panties to make a peach cobbler. AngieSaidThat Cell# 221

I picked up my pencil to write a small letter back to cell# 206.

Hey, thanks a lot. Yeah I noticed you watching me and I don't think you are crazy. I'm simply in my own lane in this place. I don't place judgments on others and if you don't mind me asking, why are you in here and what is your name?

AngieSaidThat

I jumped back on the top bunk writing to pass another hour to get to our last hour out on activity time. The women on the bottom level were out for their activity time. True enough my feelings were hurt, but

I prayed for guidance and the correct counseling from above on my sentencing turn around. I asked Jesus for guidance. My heart was opened for my purpose. I wasn't just focused on myself, I wanted to continue helping others. My path was much longer than the green mile I walked outside. I wasn't going to eat any of 3201 W. Roosevelt's cornbread that was served daily. Sometimes you can see teeth prints from the mice on the plain white light bread. Who cares? Do we deserve what the mice don't want?

I wanted to feed my spirit with scriptures and understanding from the Bible. Twelve random people were chosen and my life was placed in their hands, but I was going to feel like I had to just accept the time they chose for me. I later found out that one of the jurors were associates with the co-defendants mother. I truly felt some type of way.

Sgt. Gib returned back upstairs to key each door out so that we could have our last hour of activity time for the day. Which means the remaining of the day is lock down time. I walked over to the ice machine to get some ice. Cell# 206 walked up to me with a look in her eyes that I will never forget.

"Hey Angie, my name is Tippy. I'm in here because I killed my boyfriend. Capital Murder." She said with a deep stare in my eyes. She walked off as tears formed in her eyes. I stood there like, Wow! Speechless, as much as I talk or even a quick come back. Lost for words and thoughts.

After making a few phone calls to those I really missed and to continue trying to still get some type of events going for the LGBT Community. It really wasn't anything at the time going on for the LGBT Community. Little Rock Black Gay Pride was at a standstill. The "head nitch" was currently behind bars and very much missed. Before I knew it the hour was up. Sgt. Gib was screaming. "Lock down ladies. Everybody to your rooms and close your doors or you will miss out on your activity time tomorrow. Close your door!" He repeated, "Close your door!"

I returned to cell# 221. I got a message that my attorney friend was coming to visit me. I knew in my heart that I had to pray about our visit. I am aware that it wasn't anybody's fault but my own that I am wearing a dusty blue uniform. An addiction of any sort can take control of your spirit, but why is it that other people are able to enter into rehabilitation programs or do a few years in prison and are released. Judges are slapped on the risk and then able to become big time attorneys after addictions. Is this all based on your level of education or knowing people in higher positions?

I found myself in the most uncomfortable position trying to continue writing. My butt ached on the iron stool so I set on the bed. The conditions that most of the mats are in at 3201 W. Roosevelt are shameful.

It feels better to place soft tissue underneath your butt. The more I exercised the better. Of all the positions I tried to make myself more comfortable none of them worked. I couldn't stop my purpose in life. I decided to stand in the pill line twice a day for Tylenol to help ease the pain of the aches in my body. Can the nurse give me something to take away some of this time, I wondered. In the midst of writing my new cellmate, Mrs. Thomas, had sobered up. She finally stopped thinking she was on her way to Wal-mart. I figured once she got her food she would know her whereabouts more than ever. I politely shared my snacks with her and gave her sweets and peanut butter crackers. She pretty Much shared her life story with me. I kept her entertained with the Bible and the jailhouse conditions, which she totally agreed.

True enough, I feel as if we as inmates also have a major part to play as far as helping to keep our areas clean. On the outside of the bars most inmates probably lived as they do in jail. Some smelled worst than the zoo. Some of the officers cared enough to bring supplies from home to give to better and refreshing smells. The few days a week I am chosen to be on clean-up I could barely stand in the doorway of a few areas because of the horrible odor.

What will it hurt to get the proper disinfectant germ free cleaning supplies inside 3201 W. Roosevelt? So many people walk in these doors with some many different germs and diseases and all the inmates have to share the same toilets. I trained my body within a matter of days to receive the feeling and get use to the squat position. I felt the burning in my legs, but there was no way in hell I was going to sit on the different toilets behind the many different women with odors that smelled like something was playing hide–n-seek inside of them. My question wasn't who it was. The room revealed it! What is it that is causing the turn-up on these different odors?

I noticed every time it rained the ceilings continued to leak in some areas that caused inmates to be awakened and placed either on the lower bunks or in another cell. The back"subs" areas would flood. The thought of the much older inmates in the back weaken my stomach just Wondering if anyone on the inside or the outside cared at all. The inmates chosen for cleaned-up mopped the floors. At times with the pissy smell in the back "subs" areas I held my breath to rush a cigarette under their doors and quickly within seconds was back in the front area. Horrible!

Chapter 16

Protect Me from the Wicked

The following day my name was called by Sgt. Gib for a visit with my attorney friend, Stanley. He was a white male, sixty-one years old, 5'3", 157 lbs, with glasses sitting there with a smile on his face.

"Hello sweetheart, how are you?" He asked.

"Hello Pops, I'm already sick of this place and these women! I had a woman to show me her vagina. I've seen more of those than a gynecologist. I feel like I would be better off in the men's unit." I smiled and joked with him. We both laughed.

"Well who do you want to sign your power of attorney over to as far as the club?" He asked. "Sweetheart, I wished I had been more aggressive with you about this situation. I don't know at this point that there is too much I can do about it because you took a jury trial and caused the state money." He said. Tears instantly formed in my eyes. "Well I was scared out of a bench trial by Mrs. Copeland. It's all just a mess and I know you know enough people to turn this around. I'm ready to get out of here.   It's nasty, only two Hours out of the cell a day, sometimes less than that Stanley." Tears rolled from my eyes and my voice trembled.

"Well, Sweetheart, I can make a few calls to get you moved faster.   Yesterday was Judge Bengie Smalls's birthday.   He told me he would have given you more time, but he would've had ninety days to turn it around.   Now that a jury has convicted you it is going to be hard. Even with you and other people witnessing one of the jurors dozing off. She wasn't in a deep sleep.   I know it all sounds crazy, but it's the law and legislation.   Plus I don't write appeals or deal with them.   I am getting old.   I've beat cancer and twelve years from now I'm most likely to be dead."   He explained.

The thoughts of him saying that weakened my stomach, but to hear him repeat the statement Bengie had made pissed me off.   He may very well be a judge, but surely people talk about others even those in black robes with personal addictions.   So, is it fair to think like that about others with different addictions?

Stanley continued to talk,   "Well, Sweetheart, keep your head up.   You can call my office anytime collect.   I really can't sleep at night over this, but I know you will be running Newport."   He smiled.

"Look I know you know people in high power positions.   You are friends with everybody but President Obama and that's most likely because you didn't vote for Him." I said smiling.   We both laughed, but the truth has no defense.

"I need to get this time reduced.   I didn't understand."   I spoke clearly.

"Well, Sweetheart, here is the newspaper article that was printed in the paper.

I picked up the article and didn't read anything but the big bold black headline. I folded it up and put it in my pocket. The same way I prayed about our visit, I had to also pray on the over-rated article that I currently wasn't in the right frame of mind to read.

The two of us talked maybe ten more minutes. I hugged him and as always introduced him as my white dad to Officer Thomas.

He walked off smiling and said, "I love you." He also commented to Deputy Thomas, "Take care of the Queen Bee."

He assured the court system that I was truly the head leader of the black gay community. So, did even the newspaper use that against me? True enough most politicians hate gay people and we are surely judged by the public. We all should burn in hell for loving the same sex. Before I was locked up I stood in front of the State Capitol with Judge Gray and others on same sex marriages equal Rights. I now wonder was the outcome of being charged with aggravated robbery on facts of never being seen with a gun and never owned one. Is this justice served? The co-defendant was on probation with three gun charges. He lied and testified I gave him a toy gun. I'm sure this was at the prosecutor's urging. The honest truth is he has never had a problem getting a hold to a gun. Real talk.

True facts:

The witnesses which the State called, lied. Jo-Jo, which is Marty's, the co-defendant ex-lover, lied so much he couldn't remember any of the statement he gave to the detective six months before. The State couldn't use the other witness, Fink Tillery, to testify because he did twelve years in prison for killing his blood brother's best friend. True enough, all three of these people worked at my club and other events.

Fink has been around me for years. I helped him when he had no money. From being evicted, I put gas in his car; I paid his cell phone bills, and fed him many of hungry days and nights. He really wanted the heat off of him for impersonating a police officer. He was known for molesting teenage boys. He worked with Officer Jarvis with the Good Will program with at risk boys. I'm pretty sure he volunteered but he assured everyone that his record was expunged for doing this work. He earned a degree in Criminal Justice and as expected now knew every element of the law…lol! Fink is 5'8", 187 lbs, light skinned and Dressed as a police officer at night and wore suits in the day to fulfill his very own fantasy and sick mind of becoming a police officer. He drives a gray Impala that Jo-Jo hooked blue police lights in and carried a fake police badge.

A few weeks before 12-12-12, vice made a visit to a few of the clubs. One officer in particular, Billy Bully, who mercilessly harassed me over seven years and also wanted me to become an informant. He assured me that if I didn't tell him the name of the person impersonating a police officer that he would see to it that my club license was provoked and he would cause my business even more problems than he did in the past. Well, Officer Billy Bully accomplished that! He even called me a nigger as he continued to call my phone from a private number.

A few days later, Fink, saw Marty's picture on the news. Now mind you this is someone he just bailed out of jail and even called me asking for a hundred dollars to help with the bail, begging like he always did. He became paranoid after I told him to stay away from the club because Officer Billy Bully was out to get him. Knowing what I know now I should have let them bust his low-down dirty ass from the get-go!

The police impersonator went to the police station to give them leads and information on Marty, but asked not to be revealed. There is word for people like him. It's called a SNITCH. He knows that an informant is the closest he will get to being a police officer. My book titled *"Unfiltered"*

Tells it all.

Psalms 17:9

Protect me from the wicked people who attack me, from murders (Fink Tillery) who surround me.
They are without pity.   Listen to their boasting.   They track me down, surround me, and throw me to the ground.
They are like hungry lions, eager to tear me apart, like young lions judging, waiting for their chance.

In Jesus name.

Amen

Chapter 17

Judgment

The rain pounded against the jail and the sounds of the thunder were even louder. My prayers will never stop and my faith and hope will always play a major part in my life and purpose. My fingers continued to ache from writing faster. The lead in my pencil was always worn down and weak, but the guard respected my writing and knew that I wouldn't remain quiet at night unless they were always sharpened. A very special "thanks" to the night shift and pink beautify lips, Officer Clark. I no longer focused on the different positions to make myself comfortable to write. I simply wanted to write and make others laugh even when I didn't get the best of news. It made me feel good to uplift someone else's spirit. Why didn't the prosecutor give me that much credit before the hurricane sentencing?

I freely opened up the dictionary to read the meaning and for a clear understanding.

Judgment: The pronouncing of a formal opinion or decision; opinion of decision given.

Act of determining, as in courts, what is comfortable to law.

Justice: the decree or sentence of a court

I then read all the other words than can be used for justice...*uprightness, equitableness, fairness.*

Wow!

I'm still giving special thanks and praising GOD as I continue to walk this journey. I will continue to appeal this sentence and pray that somebody in the State of Arkansas believes in equality as it relates to punishment and grant the above meaningful words.

Judgment once played a major role in my life. I thank GOD on a daily basis for my healing from a gambling addiction, but not one time will I ever judge others. I can say this regarding the talking on the outside and behind the bars. So many will forever judge me, but I am focused only on my purpose. My vision is clear on this outcome and a lot of people that have been sentenced unfairly would not be able to be as strong as I am. Jesus had stones thrown at him, but he kept praising GOD and following his commands.

Now, that I know my purpose in life, I simply believe that justice will be served by an almighty and higher power. HE is able to do exceedingly abundantly above all that I can ask or think. And with that being said, I will not serve twelve years in Jesus name!

My setback may have made plenty of people happy and amused, but my comeback is going to confuse you! There were certain scriptures that my friend, Kim, sent me that turned up my energy on writing and laughing to freedom!

People in this place could not believe the drive I had for writing and the inner peace that I had facing so much time.

I didn't allow any of the street talk to tamper with my spirits. I prayed in the name of Jesus. To have the book thrown at you on your first felony conviction and by those that you have whole heartedly helped out of the goodness of your heart when their own family members would not help them. Pure envy and evilness. The thought of Marty's mother calling and texting me, but lying and claiming I threatened her and this woman claims to be a woman of GOD. She has even prayed with me, but stooped to any level to make it seem as if I had planned this or forced a grown man commit a crime. Funny how she never mentioned the fact the he had robbed several rich people's homes in which he was never caught. But I'm the big bad wolf? If it looks like a dog, walk like a dog, bark like a dog and eats dog food…then it's a dog, a lying dog!

AngieSaidThat

I realize that judgment and racism will always exist. I walked out the following evening and couldn't help but to notice how the Mexicans looked out for one another, no matter what. Even certain white people like Eyebrow Kecia and Amber rode it out in the same cell through it all. I Noticed my very own people are quick to say who is doing what, put others down and overall hate to see the next person rise up. I never understood why I was admired, but hated on at the same time. I realize now it's because most people envied me and wanted to be what they saw on the outside looking in. Now that I have found my true purpose I can't blame most. GOD knows who to test. HE is also the only one that can pass judgment on me at the end of the day. I'm so thankful that even with all the different crimes committed by people and all the high power business minded people that I have come in contact with on the outside and even behind the bars. I once judged others, but even in this dusty blue uniform I am able to give other people hope.

The following morning I woke up and prayed before I opened my eyes. I hopped off the top bunk and loosened the aches of my body with sit-ups. I pushed the small button on the daycare size sink about six times to get the water warmed up.   I took my small towel that we are allowed to switch out only once a week and soaped it down with my Irish Spring soap.

I always washed my towels out before using them.   The cheapness of the jail cleaning supply was a great concern of mine.   I didn't want any infections caused by the germs. Scary, Ugh!   I washed my body knowing that I wasn't going to be able to shower until evening activity hour.   I was chosen by one of my favorite deputy's, Ms. Pope, to be on clean-up.   She somehow took a liking to me and I can't explain how that happened except that she enjoyed the way I cleaned.   People once told me you have to fake it to you make it. I never had to clean anything quickly.   I hired people to clean the club and at home My Wife kept it spotless.   So is this a clean-up payback?   UGH!

Chapter 18

Tippy

I later walked outside and noticed Tippy from cell# 206 sitting alone.   She is 5'7", light skinned, beautiful smile, thick hair, long finger nails and very shy and quiet.

"Hey, how are you doing today?"   I asked.

"I'm fine and you?" she said with a beautiful smile and pearly white teeth.

"So, do you feel like you are around crazy people?"   I asked her.

"Yes, all the time." She answered and laughed.

"Listen, I don't think you are crazy, but yesterday you told me why you are in this place and I just couldn't believe it.   I could tell by the look in your eyes something just isn't right." I spoke to her very calmly.

"Angie, when I first came here I was on suicide watch. I really didn't believe that my boyfriend was gone and I'm the reason why. You know I actually called his cell phone during my first two weeks in here praying he would pick up." She spoke quietly not wanting others to hear.

"Well, do you want to talk about it?" I asked.

"I haven't talked to anyone about it, not even my attorney; I'm like really in denial." She spoke with her bottom chin trembling and in tears.

"Yeah, I can truly relate to that feeling." I explained to her what happened to me and how they really convicted me for having a gap in my teeth. We both laughed about my gap, a gap anyone could have.

We continued to talk about different crimes of others and the expected outcome, but sometimes people are convicted of the unexpected. I could tell in such a short amount of time because of her watching cell# 221. She laughed her little aching heart out listening to me. The other inmates wanted to know what could possibly be so damn funny!

I was able to breakdown the walls behind the bars in cell# 206 and break through the cries. Tippy soon warmed up to my personality and started talking to me. She had been locked up for over nine months and had never invited anyone inside her mind.

"Angie, earlier that day, I dropped two girls off over at my ex-boyfriends house. It is true that I had been stressed out some, but we worked our problems out. I picked him up that day from Wendy's. He had just started to work there."

"Tippy, how did you meet him?" I asked.

"His name was Darren. He was in truck driving school. I gave him a physical at the place where I worked. He told me I was beautiful. We talked and ended up becoming friends." She explained.

"So, what about his family and how old was he?" I asked.

"Um, he was twenty-five years old and from Mississippi. He did not have a close relationship with his family. He actually told me he hated

them. His childhood was horrible growing up and he was homeless a lot. I could relate to him. My mother moved a lot. I remember having to live in shelters and every time we moved it was always hard on me. I wasn't pretty enough to even be noticed by boys at school. My butt wasn't big enough. My hair was thick and puffy and there was this one guy, I will not ever forget his name, that made fun of me all the time until I believed the character name he gave me, "Bunka", someone I never heard of or seen before in life. From that point on I felt so bad about myself. The only time I felt pretty is when I made the dance team and was able to dance and boost up my self esteem. I started feeling like this at the age of twelve and it continued." She told me.

"You are beautiful. I'm not just telling you that, but you have to believe it from within. You have to pray for the peace to accept yourself as you are and to feel good about Yourself. To be able to feel it from within will be much more powerful than my words. You have to do something about it too, okay? Look at your smile. Girl, please!" We laughed as I continued to uplift her spirits.

"So finish telling me about your boyfriend." I asked smiling.

"I really felt sorry for him after he text me doing his three weeks of training complaining about how he hated driving trucks and the narrow roads scared him. He asked me if he could live with me until he could get another job and save some money to get his own place. I really didn't want to, but I did it anyway." She explained.

"So you moved him in and later got your groove on with the truck driver?" I asked laughing.

I wanted to make these women feel like no attorney, public defender, judge, relative, or even themselves could make them feel.

Human! Here it was I went from a club owner with a bad gambling addiction to a blue dusty uniform listening with a caring and compassionate heart. I am doing what the judge even denied me of, a con-current sentence, meaning all running together. I am happy at the same time!

She smiled, "Girl, we ended up more than just friends. I mean we really had a lot in common. We laughed together a lot. I can't just lie and say he was a bad man.

True, he had deep issues and personality changes. Sometimes I just didn't know how to take him. He also tried to commit suicide. I took him to the hospital and found out he needed professional help. I was so in love with him. He told me he wanted to go home with me, but I should have taken him to the State Hospital to get some help." The tears started rolling uncontrollably down her face. She started trembling as I looked at her.

"Listen, I know this is hard and you can talk about it later if you want too, whenever you want to vent." I told her and I meant it. I also told her to cry it out! Advice once given to me by my friend, Kim.

"Angie, I thought the detectives would just question me and release me. I have never been in jail before. They told me I was being charged with first degree murder and placed me in handcuffs. I lost it. You know I have thought about jumping over the upstairs rail several times to kill myself." She cried.

"Tippy, I have thought that too, but with my luck I will survive and just chip my two buck teeth with the convicted gap." We both laughed.

"So, how did your mom take the news? You told me how you joined the military at the age seventeen. You got married at twenty-two and both of you guys traveled the world in the military." I asked.

"Yeah, I met my husband in the military. We were both stationed in Iraq. We enjoyed life at an early age. He had issues, but we fell in love and he asked me to marry him on Christmas Day. He was twenty-seven at the time. To answer your question as far as my mom, she is very supportive. She lives in Texas and drives travel buses. She sends me money and I-Care packages and we talk often." She spoke seriously.

"So what and where did it take place that changed your life?" I asked.

"You are not going to believe it, Angie. I don't even talk to my ex-husband. He had to go back to Iraq. He came back home a completely different person. He has been diagnosed with a lot of mental issues and became very abusive. I no longer knew the man I had fallen in love with and married. I always felt like he was going to kill me one day. He is remarried now and have a good relationship with his wife. They are raising our girls. He is 100% disabled." She explained.

"Oh, so were the children around when this happened?" I asked.

"Yes, we got into an argument. We started to struggle and I stabbed him one time above his breast. I mean just one time. I didn't think I had killed him. I mean right here." She pointed on her body where she had stabbed him.

"So, did you have any bruises or scratches on you from the struggle?" I asked.

"Yes, the detectives took pictures of me." She replied.

"What did you do after you stabbed him?" I asked.

"I called my ex-husband's wife and told her." She answered. "I checked his pulse and felt nothing. I mean I really couldn't believe it. Look. I haven't told anyone this and I have already told you too much. I want to tell you the rest about that evening, but give me some time, okay?" She asked.

"Well, we have to take it one day at a time, but pray for the strength and guidance." I told her.

"Ladies, time for lock down!" The constant demands of the voices at 3201 W. Roosevelt in the crispy blue uniforms. UGH!

Chapter 19

Hot Pepper

*B*ack in cell# 221 with Mrs. Thomas, I noticed she had washed her panties out finally and hung them on the door. I couldn't believe that 3201 W. Roosevelt supplied Inmates with only one pair of panties. They were thinner than dental floss and looked like the center of a tennis racket. Pitiful! Some of the ladies looked like a blacken fish sitting inside a net. I know 3201 W. Roosevelt can do better on the underwear. I was thankful to have worn my "Hanes" and a sports bra. A hot mess!

A few hours later I took a break from writing, looked out of the window of the cell door. I noticed Tippy   in cell# 206 looking over at me smiling. Behind me in the same cell Mrs. Thomas snoozed louder and louder. I took the end of my pencil and held up her panties in the window at Tippy. I then slipped them back on the iron cell door and drew a picture of my gaped teeth and wrote the word "convicted" and held it up. Tippy laughed at me until I noticed her jaw bones trembling and obviously hurting. She rubbed her face. The fact that I was able to make her laugh at such a serious time like this facing a murder charge, being away from her girls, and the hard good-bye visits. I thought about the rainbow behind the clouds.   I know my books will become my new addiction.   I couldn't lose on this roll.

 I'm able to do something in less than two months that is very much needed behind the bars.   I am able to mentor and share laughter with those in need of it.   I'm not perfect.   I've made many bad choices in life, but I'm no longer a team player for the devil.   Trust, that when you finally put you faith in the right place, it's like oh my, my, my!   I could no longer worry about today's tests because they will be the next day's testimonies.

 I couldn't help but think about all the time I spent over the years running an unappreciated black gay club.   I am not speaking about all, but most.   Now that I am locked up I can count the people on one hand that have written me or even sent a measly five dollars.   I am reminded everyday that anyone can love you when the sun is shining.   In the storm is where you feel and learn who truly cares for you.   All my life I have been able to make people laugh. I am one of the best and well-known comedians in Arkansas.   No one is a stranger to me.   If I am able to come to jail waiting to go to prison and create unforgettable memories in less than two months, what kind of miracle am I? Untouchable by none other than my Creator!   I am blessed by the fact that you are reading my purpose, my gift, and my inner thoughts.   I am blessed with my talent and skills with paper and pencil as I insert my blessed pages inside the proper large mailing envelope to be stamped, sealed and delivered.

AngieSaidThat

 The talk soon got out about me writing a book behind the bars of 3201 W. Roosevelt.   I got the support of the inmates and employees who were all excited and wanting to purchase a copy. I sensed how so many people craved to read good stories.   I relied on the scriptures in the Bible and the *"The Mentor"* for guidance.

I couldn't speak a bit of Spanish, but the Mexicans found themselves laughing at me. The few Mexicans that didn't speak English translated by their laughter. My name Instantly became "Lesbiana", which mean lesbian in Spanish. They said it so much that I started saying it as did all the other inmates. So many nights I kept the unit laughing and the Mexicans would shout up, "Go to bed Lesbiana, we sleepy!"…LOL

I found myself listening to Roxanna. Now she wasn't someone to tell her business to anyone to quickly. She spoke English pretty well. I had just walked out of the shower and noticed a weird frown on her face. Her smile and her cute dimples lit the room up whenever she graced it in her dusty blue uniform. We even outshined some of the crispy blue uniforms. So what if they are clocking in and out and we are being counted during the standing head counts and sleeping on the hard iron bunks. Do you really know me? Checkout *"AngieSaidThat"* facebook page.

I placed my arm around Roxanna neck as she walked down the stairs.

"Hey Hot Pepper, what's the frown about and where are those dimples?" I asked.

"Angie, I'm scared to go to court in the morning. The Feds have offered me ten to life. I'm stressed out." She spoke using both Spanish and English. For a hot minute I thought, Mmh, Lesbiana, just maybe! Naw, just kidding…LOL

"Hot Pepper what are you charged with, honey?" I asked.

"One of the largest meth busts. I mean over eighty-five pounds and we also had some cocaine. I had my own personal stash of cocaine, too. My man is a big timer, you know? My Papi had so many girls." She went on to explain.

"Well damn, you are a jalapeno pepper. You are really hot! Wow!" I said and giggled.

She hit my hand, "Stop it!" She replied laughing. "No one else can ever call me Hot Pepper but you, that's it." She said laughing.

"Okay, I'm the only one that calls you that, Hot Pepper?" I teased.

"Angie, it was my man's, but they got me on a conspiracy charge." She said sadly.

Roxanna is 5'3", 155 lbs, beautiful long black hair, nice coke bottle shape body and simply beautiful. We continued talking outside until we heard one of the guards scream, "Ladies, lock it down!" I returned to my cell and wrote her a letter.

Hot Pepper,

The fact of seeing others come and go and within days are back again is hard. Sometimes we tend to turn to GOD and praying only in our times of trouble. We must continue to pray at all times through the good and the bad situations. I know you are scared about your Sentencing date. I still cannot believe that I am here, but it's true. The good thing is that I am working on what I finally realized is my purpose in life. I have hope. I have faith. I believe it and I receive it all running concurrently. So many deserve a second chance in life. That's not to say we don't deserve punishment, but not this type of time on our first convictions. Listen to me, you need to ask GOD to please rain down rain down favor on your sentencing. He has the power that no man has. He can move mountains. I'm not going to do even half of this time I've been given. My faith will release me from behind the bars. Pray for protection over your family and trust me when I say, "fear no evil." I am going to pray for you, okay Picante Hot Pepper? Good night. AngieSaidThat

Hot Pepper and I exchanged contact information. After she goes to court a few days later she will be going to Federal Prison. We talked about doing positive business ventures together. She explained to me how she missed her children. She was married for fifteen years to her high school sweetheart. He has full custody of three of her children and the fourth child lives with her mother. Her ex-husband earned over $150,000.00 a year and she was a housewife. His father passed away and left him a large inheritance. Eventually they separated but continued to have sex with each other until she met Papi, whom she fell in love with. She had never dated a Mexican before. He introduced her to cocaine and living the fast life.

She opened several businesses, drove fancy cars, had three nice homes and did whatever she chose to do in Texas. Papi made it clear to her that she belonged to him and that no one would ever come along and mess with his family. He assured her he had the hot sauce to keep the sizzle Flaming. Blow! He was much older and had never been busted. He started selling drugs at the age of sixteen.

She had over ten pounds of meth and twenty pounds of marijuana in addition to their personal stashes of cocaine traveling to Little Rock. They were pulled over and arrested, but later released by the Feds. A month or so later, whatcha gonna do when they come for you? The Feds, DEA, and Texas police raided their home that contained all the drugs. Her sixteen year old daughter knew the procedure if anything were to happen and packed three stuffed animals with money and a cell phone.

Roxanne is currently awaiting sentencing. Papi only received six years! To really be honest with you, I will never give up hope and I'm going all the way to the Supreme Court of Appeals to make right this unfair sentencing I have been given.

Chapter 20

Rea-Rea

I noticed the inmate in cell# 106 and myself usually got out on clean-up pretty much at the same time.   She reminded me so much of an old associate of mine that is currently living in Texas.   It was just something about my personality that allowed me to warm the hearts of others.   I looked over at Rea-Rea.

"Angie, I want to be in your book.   You are sweet, and girl all of these women in here want you so bad."   She said laughing with a gap between her teeth.   Rea-Rea is about 5'3", 175 lbs, her hair is parted down the center with a braid on each side.   She is currently awaiting sentencing after sitting in the county jail for three years on a murder charge.

Rea-Rea started talking, "Angie, I am going to tell you the truth about what all happened, girl.   I have had a very hard life.   I got turned out at the age of twelve.   I have seven kids. My youngest are three year old twins that are in foster care.   I wished that I had known the things that I know now." She looked at me as she was playing with her hair.

"So tell me what happened that caused you to be in here charged with first degree murder. Do you remember what took place? Do you dream about it?" I asked.

"Yes, I have dreams about it all the time and I clearly remember what happened. Girl, I think about it all the time." She explained still rubbing on her braids. "I was being taken care of by male friend who lived in the Shorter Gardens Projects. Every day I made sure he took his medication and kept his apartment clean for him at all times. Angie, I sucked his penis and gave him some of this kitty-cat." She said smiling. "He did a lot of dope, I mean a lot. He enjoyed shooting up and smoking crack." Her eyes got bigger as she explained further. "One day we got into a bad argument and I told him I was getting my things and leaving. I was going to move out. In the past when we had arguments or fights I would leave for a few days, but I always called to check on him. We started fighting. He had a knife and a hammer lying close to him. Girl, he had blackened my eyes and I just got tired of men beating on me. They had beat on me all my life. I wasn't taking anymore whippings. I have been through so much. Angie, GOD has slowed me down." She said. "I can clearly see him pushing me. He just kept pushing me. We were fighting and he hit me in the head. All I remember next is just stabbing him and stabbing him, and then it happened. I killed him. I left and went over to a friend's house. Later the police came as I was standing in the alley. He asked my name and I told him. He asked me about a few family members and then told me I had a warrant out for my arrest.

You know I have been on drugs most all of my life. I have been to the crazy house and I needed my meds." She continued talking and rubbing her head.

"Girl, quit claiming crazy meds. You will be just fine without them. Just pray about it. Have you talked to GOD about this Rea-Rea?" I asked.

"Yes, I have and to deal with the fact that I have killed someone that I really cared about haunts me every day, Angie. We really cared for each other. I mean really." She said.

"Rea-Rea, let me ask you, what made you start using drugs." I asked.

"I wanted to just fit in with the crowd. My friends enjoyed doing powder. I really didn't like it, but I did it to have fun with my friends. My other friends were boring, girl! I just wanted to fit in you know and have fun. I had a flat stomach, nice big booty, and knew how to hook a man." She said smiling.

"Angie, I remember going by Mama's house when my little nephew was only four years old and outside playing in the backyard. My daughter was only a few weeks old at the time. She is currently attending UCA now and working two jobs. I placed her in my nephew's hands and told him to sit on the porch with her until my Mama saw her. I stood behind a tree until he got to the porch and then I left to continuing doing drugs. My mother raised her to be a nice young lady. She comes to visit me with my Mama, and she even puts money on my books. Mama told me that my fourteen year old son is stubborn and out of control. I am ready for these people to offer me a deal so I can go home and help my Mama." She said with tears in her eyes.

"Rea-Rea, I know you are ready to go. Sometimes these women in here make you mad over petty things. Simply let it go and get over it. You use more energy being angry and upset versus just letting it go." I said to her.

"Well, Angie, writing will help you and it will also help many other women. We need you too in here like they need you out there. In the short time that you have been here you have opened us up to face a lot and to share our stories. Thank you! I know GOD is going to work things out for you. I can't wait until your books come out." She said and smiled. "Angie, are you really going to put me in your book?" She asked.

"Rea-Rea, I promise you I am going to put your story in the book." I assured her.

"I think GOD sent you to us for a reason. I really want to work on myself and enjoy my kids. I want all my kids to meet one another. They all need to know each other. I want to clean my Mama's house." She said smiling.

Chapter 21

Jail Life

Once I started studying the Bible, reading scriptures, and other words of wisdom, I realized that the *Face book* attention seekers, newspaper writers, and even people that I have personally helped,   and I have done things to help other club owners as well, will say and do things to make you look bad.

Where are all the articles about the good deeds I have done for the community? Where are the articles about all the fundraisers I have had to raise money for rent and utility assistance for HIV & AIDS infected people of the community, for burial expenses for families that didn't have insurance or money to bury their loves ones, for back to school drives for families that couldn't afford supplies for their children, for food and toy drives to give to families that I didn't even know at Christmas time, and for mentoring the youth?   Where are the newspaper articles about me helping to campaign for candidates at election time?

Where are the articles about me being a leader of the LGBT community, and for being one of the funniest and very well-known comedians of Little Rock, Arkansas? Once AngieSaidThat graces a stage, the name is never forgotten!

Yes, I can admit I battled a gambling addiction, but that's no different than the judges that have been busted for doing cocaine. They most likely only get a slap on the hand and then step down to become attorneys. I have never owned a gun or ever been seen with a gun, but yet I am charged with aggravated robbery and facing twenty-one years in prison.

I have gone from a popular and very well known club owner and comedian to a prisoner being introduced the hoe squad and Little Debbie Snack Cakes. So, I ask is justice always served properly?

The state legislatures need to make changes to the laws of our penal system versus enforcing old laws that have been around since the turn of the century. I deserve punishment, but to serve twenty-one years for aggravated robbery when I have never owned a gun or ever been seen with a gun? Plus the jury was not a jury of my homosexual peers. They did not understand the gay lifestyle and I'm sure they disagreed with it in itself. Most people think we as gays should burn in hell anyway. The real truth of the matter is ineffective counsel.

Surely, if the Jews threw stones at Jesus and took him to jail and yet GOD made a way for him to be freed, I am no different and I have faith that He can make a way for me too! The more I thought about it the more determined I became to become a writer to get my story all the way to the Supreme Court, the members of the State Legislature, or Someone that GOD will place upon their hearts to open up the doors even for me.

The inmates supported my movements on writing about our real life stories and experiences. I walked around amongst murderers, child molesters, child abusers, arsonists, mentally ill people that really needed to be in a mental hospital, drug dealers, drug addicts, and robbers. But, we are all human and have stories to tell too. We have stories to tell about the conditions of the jail. The heavy dust, the mice, the mildew, the nets in the showers, the disgusting crap all over the walls, the disgusting food, and the list continues. We have stories to tell about the employees and the way some of them mistreat the inmates and make them feel less than human. The employees have to work in the conditions of the jail that the inmates are forced to live in. Most employees will not speak up about the horrible conditions of their workplace because it would put their jobs in jeopardy. If the inmates spoke up it could lead to an inmate riot and a major write-up for us. 3201 W. Roosevelt County Jail is in need of some major changes and upgrades.

It's worth writing about to let people know the conditions of the county jail even though some people think they will never have to deal with it. But, you never know what may come your way. You don't know what the future holds.

I hate it that the rotating officer on duty came into the unit tonight looking like Lionel Ritchie with an upgraded haircut. Officer White is 5'8", light skinned, 170 lbs, and worked the "B" shift.

"Look, for the first sixty days I stuck with the same clean-up. I pick the ones that I already know in here and you're new." He said to me.

I looked at him and said. "Look Bro, don't let the dusty blue uniform fool you. It's your choice who you pick to be on your clean-up. I'm trying to ask you about moving to another cell. Do I look like I'm stressing about serving ice, or mopping and scrubbing nasty showers? You should pick the ladies that you want for clean-up duty. If I was the deputy I would choose who I wanted too, Bro."

"Well, I am not moving you. I have no reason to move you. I just got back from being off on suspension and you need to grow up." He said as he walked off.

I thought to myself, this lemon-head look-a-like young bastard was just rude to me for no reason. I am someone he is not familiar with or want to guard. I made sure he knew I wasn't the reason he was suspended and I realized he wasn't the reason I was locked up. It just made no sense how some of the deputies packed their problems along with their lunch bags and brought them to work to inflict on the inmates. Ugh! I had to remember to remain humble.

I was moved out of cell# 221. An associate I knew from the outside named Charlene got arrested on three counts of domestic abuse. She cried, cried, and cried as she talked to Deputy Herring who was working the "A" shift. Deputy Herring was one of the officers that you didn't ever want to go home. She is really sweet and went by the rules and guidelines as well. No one minds giving respect to someone that will respect you inside or outside of jail. When Charlene looked up and spotted me she screamed my name and reached out to hug me.

"No hugging." Deputy Herring said.

"Look, can I please go in the cell with Angie?" She asked and cried with her long Brazil hair and eyelashes that were all slippery and wet. She is very attractive. I met her at Jazzi's Night Club on Asher Avenue. I remember hanging out with my blonde head stud brother, B'Nutt. We both thought she was flawless.

I moved downstairs to cell# 104. She stopped crying and explained that she had a fight with her sister and slapped her sister's fourteen year old twins. Supposedly the sister ran off with $40,000.00 of her money.

She continued talking. "I can't believe I am in a cell with you. I want to take a picture in our blue uniforms." She went from crying to smiling and said. "Angie, I'm cold. Do you have a t-shirt and socks?"

I pulled out a thermal shirt and a pair of socks for her. Before I knew it, some inmates from the top level came to my door complaining about me leaving from upstairs. Every few seconds a different face came to the door, even the Mexicans. I instantly felt bad, but at the same time, I felt good about making Charlene's tears disappear. She asked me about my charges. I simply told her that my gambling addiction got the best of me. I stopped my habit, but the charges were like a nightmare. She couldn't believe that I had received so much time since I have never owned or ever been seen with a gun. She asked me how was it that my spirit remained the same and how was I able to be so humble. My answer was simple. I have faith in GOD and I have hope that I will get an early release.

I shared with her that I respected the deputy's positions, but a few of them were just rude because of the uniform they wore and the little authority they have. Some of the deputies simply went overboard.

Most of us in these blue dusty uniforms have lived great lives. Anyone can get caught up in a bad situation or make wrong choices or decisions.

"Do you know how well known you are on the outside of this place? And I see the people in here really like your spirit." She said.

I turned around and looked at her and said. "Look, I am fully aware of my popularity. I have no excuse and the truth needs no defense. I gambled to ease a lot of pain, hurt, And stress. Nobody could ever tell what was hidden behind the laughter, but I continue to openly pray for healing as I have been blessed to do. Even behind these bars. This is no longer my battle. It's the Lord's. I'm now focused on my purpose now and forever. So, I cannot and will not worry about what the next person think or have to say about my life."

She touched my arm and said. "Angie, you are so humble and blessed."

"Yes, I am humble and I am blessed. You will be going to court on Monday and don't stress over it. Be thankful. You are going to be just fine, okay?" Maybe you need to get some anger management help and please know that money is the root of all evil. It's not worth it and AngieSaidThat!"

"You right! Hey, will you write something for me on a piece of paper to show I was in your cell with you? I got a chance to see T.I., the rapper. He was locked up with my brother." She asked.

I laughed and said. "I got you, but I am not that famous yet."

She assured me that she wanted to stay in touch and write. I explained to her that I really didn't expect things from people. The word "expectation" alone means Expecting; anticipation. I simply keep my mind on my purpose and vision of writing.

After talking to her and making a few phone calls, time seemed to pass quickly. She took her pills from the nurse and I fixed her a peanut butter and jelly sandwich. We laughed and she soon passed out.

My pencils were in need of sharpening. They were getting even smaller and I could barely write. It was time for another shift change. Deputy Clark was nice, dark skinned, hot pretty pink lips, and very handsome. I noticed the inmates watching him. I needed my pencils sharpened and when I could no longer write, I screamed.

"Deputy Clark, will you please let me sharpen my pencils?"

He continued writing on his log sheets so I asked again. "Bubble Gum Lips, I see these women looking at you, Brotha. I need my pencils sharpened so I can write.   Look over at bunk 16, she's looking at those lips."

The women laughed.   I looked out of the small window on the door and I could clearly see the deputy's station.   Deputy Clark looked up and smiled.

Bunk 16 was reserved by none other than Red.   She's currently waiting to appear in court on charges of rape.   She had just gotten off probation for the same charges with a seventeen year old.   Now this child is only thirteen years Old.   Baby, Nancy Grace, needs to be here at 3201 W. Roosevelt, but AngieSaidThat has live coverage behind the bars with the story from Lady Red.

A few days ago I asked her what happened and she explained. "Angie, I was actually walking with my kids and I saw him watching me.

He really didn't look thirteen.   He is taller than I am, has a deep voice, and is very nice looking.   He approached me. "

Lady Red is a black female, 5'8", 175 lbs, red hair, light skinned, and had a lot of hair bumps under her chin as if she shaved.

I asked.   "So, you had no clue of his age and that he was underage."

"I didn't know he was thirteen years old."   She answered.

"How do you know this kid?"   I asked.

"I know his family.   He came on to me saying he had been watching me.   He told me he wanted to hook-up and I told him to stop playing."   He joined me as I was walking with my kids.   We talked and a few days later we had sex."   She said.

"Red, at that age is he fully aware of what to do and was he even working with anything?"   I asked.

"He got it going on, Angie. I really didn't think he was that young performing sex like that. He started texting me every day and I would reply back. It got to the point that his Daddy started bringing him over to my house to have sex with me. I slept with the Daddy a few times too, but I fell in love with the son. Then his mother somehow found out and called me. She told me if I gave her $50.00 she wouldn't press charges against me. I didn't have $50.00 at the time. Angie, he is in love with me. I didn't rape him. He did all the work." She explained.

"Hold on Sister, you mean to tell me she asked you for $50.00? I asked.

"Yeah." She replied.

"What if you had gotten pregnant by this boy?" I asked.

"I would have blamed it on the Daddy." She answered.

"Why do you prefer young boys?" I asked.

"I don't know. I wished I would have stayed with my kid's father. He's my age, thirty-one. The detectives questioned him and his Mama showed them the text messages." She said looking at me.

"What did the detectives say?" I asked.

"He asked me about us having sex. How it started. When, where, and how many times." She answered.

"Ugh!" I mumbled.

"Last time I got probation and I'm hoping that's what I get this time." She said.

"Well, who knows?   Look at what I am facing and there are some stories that I've listened to and some people come back with just that, probation.   But you really need to get someone you own age.   It's sad and not worth it on the real.   You have kids of your own and that's not a good feeling.   I have nieces and nephews and to hear this weakens my heart and spirit.   It's not cool at all.   I am not judging, but I don't like this story at all.   Hey, whatever this illness or evil spirit is in you, you need to pray to be delivered from it.   Okay?"   I calmly told her.

"You right and I am going too."   She replied.

The devil is truly busy, Mr. Clark walked over to bunk 16 to return my pencils, Lady Red, watched him like a fat woman watching the slice of cake of her choice.   She walked over to get the pencils and to get a closer look at him.   She licked her lips as she returned with my half sharpened pencils.

I screamed through the door.   "Deputy Clark, you better look up her charges, Brotha!"   We all laughed and I Continued to write.   Red even cracked up laughing because she was not expecting me to call it out.

The unit was quiet as I looked at the clock.   It was 3:30 AM. My fingers were hurting due to the size of the small pencils.   I am thankful I have the energy to write, but I needed to rest.

Chapter 22

The Newspaper Article

The respect that I got from the inmates and others that simply listened to me talking to others touched me. The women in different areas of the jail were even screaming.

"Angie, can you call my public defender? Can I get some chips? I have been to your club. Are you single?" It seems as if the questions never ended.

Many days and evenings the inmates asked me to come outside and perform a comedy show. There were times when I wanted to cry, but I found myself making someone else laugh or sharing words of wisdom with them. I still couldn't stop thinking about the lady that died only doors down from me. I know that if GOD calls his children home there is nothing anyone can do. We are not to question GOD. He does not make mistakes.

A change can't hurt anyone that's imprisoned.   If the system would just take advice from a person who is living within the system, or even from someone on the outside that has been in the system, changes and conditions inside the system could be greatly improved.

I finally decided to share the newspaper article written about me with the other inmates.   They respected   me so much that I forgot sometimes that I was an inmate too in the dusty blue uniform and orange shower shoes.   I was known in the streets for my swagger and my fashions.   I was a great dresser.   I have taken photos with Da Brat, Fantasia, Frankie (Keyshia Cole's mother), Phyllis Yvonne Stickney (*What's Love Got To Do With It   &   New Jack City*),   Furonda (*America's Next Top Model*),   Eddie Griffin, Lavelle Crawford, Bruce Bruce, and Ricky Smiley.   These people have either been to my club or I have performed with them in comedy shows.   My personality and my talent ain't no joke!

I honestly feel like GOD is not pleased with me for being here in the county jail, but I know he loves me and has forgiven me for my sin. Nor is he pleased with my ineffective counsel and the amount of time I unjustly received.   I would have never agreed to a jury trial if I had been advised properly and if I had fully understood the law and how a jury trial worked.   I would've just had a bench trial with a judge who has expertise of the law versus a jury trial.

To receive and read such an article written about me by John Lynch of the *Arkansas Democrat Gazette* was disheartening.

Nightclub Owner Found Guilty of   '12 LR Bank Robbery

A Little Rock woman who claimed to be the victim of mistaken identity was convicted Wednesday of being the female bandit who peppered-sprayed a bank clerk during a December 2012 armed robbery.

Angela Richardson was sentenced to 21 years in prison by an eight-woman, four man jury that deliberated less than two hours after a two day trial before Pulaski County Judge Bengie Smalls.

The 43-year-old nightclub owner was found guilty of aggravated robbery and theft. She'll have to serve about 12 years before she is eligible for parole.

Richardson said she was with relatives when the Metropolitan National Bank on Cantrell Road in Little Rock was robbed by a man with a gun and a woman who pepper-sprayed a teller and escaped with about $2,000.00.

Her lawyers, Jeannie Copeland and Kim Burrows, said the woman robber was a cross-dressing man.

The female robber's face was seen briefly in the bank-surveillance video, but that fleeting glance at a camera was captured in a still photograph by police. The defense and prosecution clashed over whether the picture was Richardson.

"This picture looks like a man." Copeland said in her closing statement. "Angela Richardson was not in the bank on that day."

While cross-examining Richardson, Sonia Davis, the deputy prosecutor held a photo up to the woman's face and asked jurors whether Richardson shared the robber's distinctive gapped teeth.

"That is not me." Richardson told the jurors. "That doesn't look anything like me."

The bank teller, Carter, picked Richardson out a photographic lineup and testified that he thought the woman robber was wearing a wig. Getting sprayed in the face was the worst pain he has ever suffered, he also told the jurors. The robber sprayed him even though he was following her command to turn over the money, he said.

Also identifying Richardson as the robber was her co-defendant, 25 year-old Marty Junior, who testified that the holdup was Richardson's idea and that she had supplied him with a toy gun that he used. He said he worked as a bouncer for Richardson at her Club Good Times on Asher Avenue.

He said he'd gotten $400 from the holdup, but he gave $200 back to Richardson who said the money would be used for a lawyer "just in case."

In exchange for his cooperation, Junior, was allowed to plead guilty to robbery, reduced from aggravated robbery, and felon possession of a firearm with a 35-year prison sentence that will keep him behind bars for at least eight years.

Jo-Jo Smith of Louisiana, a close friend of Junior's, testified that he'd also been a bouncer at Club Good Times and that Richardson had been looking for someone from club security to help her rob a bank the weekend before the Metropolitan holdup. He said he recognized her on the surveillance video.

Testifying on Richardson's behalf was her sister, Monique, who said Richardson had been with her teenage son and elementary-age daughter at the time of the bank robbery. The son, Adrein, confirmed that account, saying Richardson was with him until late afternoon.

In closing arguments, deputy prosecutor, Martique Hopkins, (New Jack City prosecutor look-a-like) told the jurors none of the prosecution's witnesses had a reason to lie about Richardson.

But all of Richardson's witnesses - connected to her by love, blood, or employment- had a motive to cover up for the defendant, Hopkins said.

"She is going to say or do anything within her power to get you guys to find her not guilty," the deputy prosecutor said.

The Metropolitan holdup wasn't the first time Richardson was accused of a bank robbery. She was acquitted of a 2003 bank robbery, also saying she was mistakenly identified.

Court records show she was a suspected, but never charged, of being a pepper-spraying woman robber who worked with a male accomplice to hold up another Cantrell Road bank in 2003.

I received the article in jail from my attorney friend, Stanley. After I read it, I placed it in my uniform shirt pocket. A day later I took it out and placed it inside a book.

A very powerful and faith filled book titled *"The Purpose Driven Life"*.

People asked if I was mad about the article. I thought about it for a minute and that minute turned into a week. I was then able to answer truthfully when Tippy asked me again outside.

"I'm going to say this. I am a comedian at heart. I crack jokes on people all the time. The fact is the person who wrote this article is just doing his job. I actually wrote him a letter, but flushed it down the toilet.

No, I am not mad because I can take criticism from people. A lot of people can't handle criticism from others, but I can dish it out and I can take it. They are all aware of how well-known I am in the public and wanted to prove a point. The thing is this, he's writing for the newspaper, but I'm behind the bars fulfilling my purpose and writing for AngieSaidThat readers that will read and enjoy my books. I know that everything listed in the court records, reported on the news, or written in newspapers aren't always true facts. I was told by the judge over my trial that my statements were "he say, she say" regarding Jo-Jo saying Marty stole his gun.

If I had planned this, wouldn't I know all the people involved? Marty clearly stated that he called a friend of his to assist in the robbery. This friend also has a gap in his teeth. The photo clearly shows someone with a gap and a mustache.

I was the driver, but I was convicted by the gap in my teeth. Did all the threats come from the third person, but Marty and Jo-Jo flipped it all on me at the last minute? The newspaper stated I gave him $400.00, but took $200.00 back for attorney fees. Wow! People wonder why I call 12-12-12 the nightmare from hell. So many lies were told under oath. The truth is I drove the car and never said a word about Marty's boyfriend who was inside the bank with him. The boyfriend, Marty, and Jo-Jo were doing the remix to the movie *"Brokeback Mountain"*.

So many lies were told and I was pretty much numb during the two day trial. Sitting here in jail now and thinking about just how improperly I was advised is sad, but it is true.

12-12-12 now has me facing twelve years in prison. I finally copied and wrote the article in my book and then I flushed it down the toilet with something else that belongs in the toilet. Bullshit! Pure bullshit!

After talking to the ladies outside, I went in and jumped back on the top bunk to continue writing. I quietly prayed to keep my faith, spirit, and hope alive. I asked my Creator to please give me an understanding on the amount of time I was sentenced to and deliverance from an unjust sentence. I opened up the New Testament to Hebrews 12 to pray about the 12 years which backwards is 21 years. 12-12-12 ...the nightmare from hell!

~ GOD's Discipline Proves His Love ~

"My child, don't ignore it when the Lord discipline you, and don't be discouraged when he corrects you. For the Lord disciplines those he loves and he punishes those he accepts as his children."

After talking to Tippy and reading the Bible to lift up and maintain my spirit, I thought about what she told me while we were outside. She explained to me how some women, including herself, were here on murder charges. She also explained that most of the women really felt comfortable telling me the truth about what really took place at the time of their crimes. She said that my sense of humor and the fact that I was wearing the same dusty blue uniform as they were made it easier for them to open up to versus talking to a private attorney or a public defender, who are strangers to their hearts. I wanted to make these ladies heart beat again and more so not be brokenhearted about the reasons they are behind the bars. We are truly reminded of the whys and the why-nots on a daily basis. My heart wanted to help and listen. I wanted others to be aware of the many types of addictions, the consequences of making wrong choices and decisions, and surrounding yourself with the wrong people just to fit in, the importance of safe sex, that we deserve upgrades and better conditions inside the jail. I spoke with the young ladies about personal hygiene. We do not have to smell and look like we are in jail. My jail house cologne lotion was talked about daily. I made sure the young ladies of the LGBT community shaved their most important areas and maintained themselves as the women they were born as.

A few days ago, as I was waiting for the shower, I noticed one of the inmates named Bri, from cell# 228, getting out of the shower. She had on her pants and a sports bra. I noticed that under her arms it looked like she had Buckwheat in the headlock. She had so much nappy hair under her armpits.

"Bri, now look nephew, you got to shave that hair from under your arms, sweetheart, and I can only imagine what's sitting in those boxers. Listen, hair holds odors and that's why you stay musty, nep. Here, take some of this cologne lotion I have created and rub it on your body. Did you order a razor?" I asked.

"Yeah, I ordered one." She answered and smiled.

"Good, make sure you shave all the hair off your private parts or trim it as low as possible. And shave under your arms too. Nep, I might have to call the state's lawn service for your under arms." I said and we both laughed.

"Angie, I'm going to shave. I promise." She said looking like Ricky Smiley.

"I am going to write you a note and trust me when I'm finished with you, you will have a reason to smile even more. I see you have nice fresh white shoes and white t-shirts and you must smell fresh too, okay, playa?" I told her.

"Okay, Angie, don't forget to write me." She said as she rubbed on some of my cologne lotion and walked away smiling.

I jumped in the shower thinking as usual. I needed to find away to get my thoughts to the right people. I continued to write the judge, but being that he was also a friend of my attorney friend, I knew that he had said he would have given me more time if he could have. I have never been before him in his courtroom and I really don't understand why he feels that way towards me. I'm sure he has personal issues of his own.

Why do some people think they are more powerful than GOD himself? I will find a judge that will show mercy and give me a fair reduced sentencing or someone in the system will step up and need me to help and mentor others. My hope and my faith assures me of this.

I walked back to cell# 221 and sat on the hard iron stool to write Bri a letter.

Bri,

Nep, I know that I can talk to you. I'm not perfect and never claimed to be. Even Jesus got stoned down for helping the people. I'm trying to be a mentor to the LGBT younger generation and I know we must continue to pray with faith and have hope in order to receive it. Our creator has a way of working things out. All things are possible with GOD. The fact is we are already being judged because of our lifestyle and we must stay positive around here, okay?

We must try our best to look decent and smell good around all these sensitive and nosy ladies. Even if it takes ordering men deodorant, cocoa butter lotion, and Vaseline off the commissary list. Nep, what's the use of having new shoes and fresh white t-shirts and socks, but not taking care of your personal hygiene? You always keep a pack of cigarettes, so after brushing your teeth, get some Jolly Ranchers to freshen you breath before you conversate with others. We are in jail, but we don't have to look like we are in jail. Stay fresh Lil Rickey Smiley look-a-like and let's make it count. Nep, once you get out of here, please stay out!

Hey, shave and save the talk on shower calls.

Much Love,

AngieSaidThat!

I'm sure people have teased and bullied Bri a lot. She is about 5'4", 120 lbs, short natural hair, a gap in her teeth, and looks a lot like the comedian Rickey Smiley. She has a great personality, but no manners whatsoever. She explained to me that she has been in and out of jail since the age of fifteen. She is twenty years old. She told me how she wanted to change her life and better herself. I advised her to go back to school and to talk to someone about her behavior issues. She is capable of doing anything she wants to do, but I simply feel like she wants to fit in with other people and feel loved.

Speaking of love, tonight I was one of the five people chosen for clean-up. We all walked outside for a little break while waiting on the pill call to finish up. It was Toe-Toe, Manda, Candy, King, and me. As always, I had to give the ladies something to laugh about.

King started talking. "Angie, look at my arms. Listening to you gives me chills and I want to be in your book. I lost my mother a few years ago. She was forty-eight years old. We both used crack. I have two children and my youngest is by my pimp. He has been around my family since before I was even born. He is seventy-one years old and we have a son together."

"Hold on girl, stop lying." I said.

"Nah, I'm not lying. He comes to see me every Sunday." She continued. "Look, I love to sing and I pray that someone will discover me by my singing." She said.

King is about 5'7", 145 lbs, short braided hair and she is cute. She really reminds me of a true tom-boy. I thought she preferred women, but I learned better as she continued to talk.

"Angie, I was seriously involved with a man who works for the City of Little Rock. It was like love at first sight. He opened the doors for me. No one has ever done that for me. Most people like me that are on drugs, just wants to be loved. I smoked an eight-ball a day and was trying to put one in me. This particular night I had twenty dollars and was hanging out at the barbershop where he served most of the time. I really couldn't even think about the dope due to the fact that he opened the door for me to get into the car with him. From that night on we were together every day after he got off work. He would meet me at the barbershop. I went from smoking an eight-ball a day to a gram a day." She explained.

"So, King, why are you in here?" I asked.

"KT, the one you talked to and helped out, I stabbed her mother in the face. She has eighty-six stitches." She replied.

"What! Are you kidding me? Why?" I asked. I just couldn't believe it.

"He's her boyfriend, too. We both fell for him and we lived only two blocks away from each other. Some months later all three of us got into a fight. She pulled out a stun gun on me and all I could see was blue. I was five months pregnant with his child and all I know is that I blacked out and sliced her up. I wasn't looking for any trouble. He came over to my house crying and saying he wanted to work things out. We got to fighting and she walked up at 4:00 AM in the morning. And yes, I wanted a hit and he served me. I left the scene after I sliced her up. I knew her face was split wide open. He called the police. They later issued a warrant for my arrest and I'm charged with aggravated assault. I lost my baby in here. I bled for days and all the deputies asked me was why was I using so many pads. They counted the number of pads I used. I prayed to GOD to ease my pain and eventually I didn't feel any more pain." She said as tears formed in her eyes. "I continued to do standing head count. I honestly believe my baby had been dead for over five days. They finally took me to the hospital and I stayed in there for eight days. Do you know they never called a Code Red? I felt bad, but, you know what, Angie, I am glad we got a chance to meet. I don't go to clubs, but I do read and feel like your book is going to touch a lot of people." She said as we shook hands.

"Well, I truly hope so, and it's like this King, I can't say it's going to be easy around here, but don't put all your faith in any judge. Pray that GOD guides the judge's heart or touch someone else that really cares about us. So, with you being older, have you spoken to KT about what you did to her mother's face and apologized to her?" I asked.

"Yes, I have talked to her about it. She told me that she is not close to her mother." She answered.

"King, I can't sit here and say that I could face someone who has damned near taken my mother's face off. I guess because my mother and I had a very close relationship. She passed in 2000. So, maybe it is different between them, but she still loves her mother. So, even if you have to write her a small letter, just tell her that you have prayed about it and both of you guys were sick from the addiction of drugs. Sometimes, the spirits of demons gets the best of us in the midst of things that controls us other than our Creator." I said.

"Angie, you are so right and I had no plans on stabbing her and I hate that it is KT's mother. I really like KT. She is really a sweet person, but she feels like she has no one to turn to. She got caught up into the neighborhood gangs looking for love," She explained.

"Yeah, I look out for KT. She is a sweetheart. She's young and needs guidance and we all want that unconditional love. I've always had it, but when you find your purpose, it's called having self-esteem and being thankful." I said.

We continued to talk about how people just want to feel loved. I started telling her about how so many people get caught up in "gay families" just wanting unconditional love, but end up just dividing the community with the drama. Something I will never miss is the "gay family" beefing. I hope and pray that the younger generation find something positive to get into instead of joining families and all the negativity that comes with it.

The younger deputy on duty walked out and told us to come inside. We all finished with our clean-up and took showers. They went back out to get their last smoke of the night. I looked at the time and it was ten minutes to 9:00 PM.

The older deputy on duty tonight, Ms. Frown Brown, got on every single person's nerves in the entire unit. She is one of those people that really hated her job, but had probably been working at the same place year after year. Some of the deputies feel as if they can treat the inmates any type of way, and she is no different. As people we all must be reminded on a daily basis that somebody loves you. And that somebody is Jesus, even if no one else does. We expect so much out of family members and friends. We sometimes find out later that everyone isn't really a friend. I've learned not to expect anything from anyone, but I will continue to share my blessings with the few that have stood by me. And sometimes that does not include family. Yes, it hurts, but it is nothing that prayer can't change.

I almost allowed Deputy Frown Brown (Lock 'em Down) to get into my spirits, as I watched her deny other inmates who were simply asking for a cup of ice, or to call a bondsman, or a family member. It really saddens me to know she had eaten everything she wanted to and crave for, but was denying the inmates ice. She is solid as a rock! If an inmate had two of the 9 oz cups, she would take one away and say. "Why you looking like that? You are only allowed one cup and do I look like I am afraid of you? Get your chow and go up to your cell. Next! Make sure everything is on your tray and keep the line moving. I need y'all to keep a straight line and no talking." She frowned and talked at the same time.

I was standing and servicing ice not too far from her. The thought of these women that didn't know and are really too afraid to ask the deputy's any questions because they are so rude for no reason at all. They act as if a set of jailhouse rules come inside the Action Packs with the small half size toothbrush, generic brand toothpaste and very small piece of white soap that the jail gives us. Really! I mean some of these ladies body odors are unbearable and one piece of soap was not going to do the trick for some of these women. One inmate even had the nerve to shower and lie out in the sun trying to tan. Doll Baby, are you serious!

Not even three days later, an inmate name Britney was placed on suicide watch and I wasn't surprised. She tried to cut herself with the razor we ordered from commissary to shave with. Britney was a twin. She is over three hundred pounds, 5'4", pale, has black hair and smells like she belongs in the Arkansas State Fair with the horses playing hide and go seek. I really believe she couldn't find the odor. It had to be hiding in some of those hidden places.

Once, you are placed on suicide watch you are escorted to a room and ordered to take off all of your clothes. You are given a green piece of thick fabric with snaps on the shoulders in order to secure it. It is pretty much a thick green hospital gown, but the inmates call it a turtle suit. I noticed Britney standing in the window waiting to shower. I swear she looked as if she was waiting for a large group of people to hang Christmas ornaments all over her. As much as I tried not to, before I knew it I had tears running down my face from laughing so hard. I was too tickled!

Chapter 23

My Letters

Here are some of the types of letters I received as an inmate behind the bars:

"Angie Richardson, also known as AngieSaidThat, is our friend, our sister, our loved one! She has been portrayed unjustly. This is a person that

would give you her last. She has helped support many. She has been the backbone for the LGBT community. She is known for her voice and hilarious character. She is proud of who she is and encourages everyone to be themselves. To be who they are. A comedian at heart and she is never a dull person. If you knew Angie, you would love her because to know her is to love her. A voice like hers must be heard and she made sure

Of it, but her heart is bigger than her mouth and those who truly know her knows that!"

Free AngieSaidThat!

Another letter…

I was eighteen years old when I personally and openly embraced my sexuality. There were the obvious fears that I was faced with. Will my parents, siblings, family and friends still love and accept me? Will I be an outcast? Is there anyone else feeling like me and just as scared as I am? I stuck to online forums where I could anonymously be myself. It was on those sites that I learned of the openly gay black women who owned a club here in Little Rock for the LGBT community. I was more afraid than I have ever been going to her club for the first time. What if someone seen me? It was Club Goodtimes. I saw so many people. All races, genders, preferences, and ages that were just like me. There was so much pride, peace, and comfort inside the club. Club Goodtimes felt like home to me. Within those four walls I felt like I could remove the mask that I was forced to wear by society who says my lifestyle is formed by an embarrassing abomination. I was able to be somebody. I'd been fighting myself to be myself. I personally give thanks and much appreciation to Angela Richardson for making that possible. No one else had enough courage, strength, and dedication to the local LGBT community to give us somewhere to go and just come together in unity. It may not have been for initial vision or intent to have her name and face be so big and influential in the gay community. But that's just who she became. To go from a party promoter to an entrepreneur, author, and a comedian is pretty remarkable and amazing. Angela (AngieSaidThat) Richardson, became well known over the years. I'd only had a weekend club owner impression of Angie. It wasn't until three years ago that I was given the privilege to be personally introduced to this magnificent local celebrity type of woman. Just like anyone else who meets someone that's in the public eye, I tried to find flaws in her that she wasn't as glamorous as most portray her to be. She is just as humble, loving, giving, and peaceful person behind doors as she is in the public view. That being said, I cannot accept the sentence that was dished out in the courtroom on Wednesday, June 4, 2014. I'm a dedicated voter. I'm a strong woman overall and I believe it is not over until GOD says it is over. We will not accept this defeat. The court may have been adjourned, but this is far from over.

Shaneika

I laid on the top bunk deeply thinking and asking myself even after overcoming a bad gambling addiction after so many years, is this what you get in return or is it just me? I had to take this to the Supreme Court without a doubt. Too many people wanted me to be successful, but double the amount wanted me to fail. It wasn't about who had to say what or what others thought or wanted. It is all about my purpose in life and fulfilling the gifts and talents that were instilled in me. I was finally ready to hit "the play button!" I placed my dusty blue uniform pants under me and laid back on my mat to continued writing. Everyone else was sleeping. I finally got the peace I needed to please my Creator.

I didn't hear any one screaming, "I need a flush" or "Standing head count". I even calmed the pregnant lady in cell# 701 down by giving her a bag of chips and some Vaseline to help her itching. She screamed louder than people on a roller-coaster ride. The men weren't banging on the walls or inmates talking through the jail toilets. All I could hear at this moment were the keys jiggling as the guard made rounds.

I listened to my cellmate on the bottom bunk sleeping peacefully. She talked to herself a lot in her sleep, but this was her third strike so far with me as a cellmate. I knew her somewhat from the outside. Drugs had messed her up pretty bad, but she loved reading the Bible. She still found Jesus and made sure that I read the scriptures that she felt were written just for me. She made sure my socks, t-shirts, and thermals were always cleaned. She would get that little white bar of soap and go over to that small sink and baby when I tell you Fun Wash or a dry cleaners ain't got nothing on her, you better mark my words!

I made sure I put in for a visit to the barbershop to keep my hair freshly lined and I "whited it out" at 3201 W. Roosevelt. Even behind the bars I kept my appearance on point. The younger inmates gave me the fruit from their trays. I would squeeze it into my lotion and rub it on my body after taking a good shower with my Irish Spring soap. Even the Mexicans were like, "O La Me so horny!" I'm the fresh fruity favorite on Friday's.

AngieSaidThat

July 3, 2014

    I was pretty sad calling my baby knowing that it was Meaka's, my baby sister, birthday and I was unable to be with them.　But just to hear their voices and to make them laugh even over the phone meant more to me than having a slice of birthday cake.　Truth be told, I had a lot on my mind, but I can't really explain the feeling I had inside after sitting in jail for only a month and facing twenty-one years.　I can only explain it day by day.　So, until standing head count at the jailhouse wake-up call from Sgt. Gib.　Goodnight.　I need a flush.　Ugh!

Happy 4th of July!

    It was standing head count time.　"I need everybody at your bunks and standing."　Sgt. Gib screamed at fifteen minutes to 7:00 AM. To be honest, I laid on my bunk and simply looked up at him to let him know I was alive.　I prayed and just laid in the bunk wishing I could just put all of this behind me.　But, everyday there is a friendly reminder as to where I am.　"I need a flush!" Some of the women screamed after eating too many beans.　"Fire in the hole!", "Emergency flush!" Ugh!

    I just wanted to go back to sleep and dream about whatever came to me other than thinking about sitting in a dusty blue uniform on a hard bunk in a jail cell.　My cellmate didn't skip a beat when it came to waking up for early morning chow.　I told her not to wakea me up asking for my tray.　Every woman in the unit knew not to wake me early asking me for nothing.　I told all of them that unless Oprah Winfrey came asking for me, do not think about waking me up over some oatmeal that looked like it has been squeezed on top of cornbread or what they claimed to biscuits.

    A few hours later even with all the noise going on, I heard Sgt. Gib calling for activity time. The thought of being away from My Wife and family members really had me wanting to just sleep the day away. I decided to stay in a few more minutes longer.

"Angie, we want you to come outside with us. Get up and come out of this cell, please! " Tippy said as she stood smiling and looking through the small window on the door.

"Okay, give me a few minutes to get myself together." I replied.

My cellmates made up so much noise until it was impossible for me to go back to sleep. The men were banging on the walls again and talking loudly to other inmates. It was so much easier for me to retreat my mind after midnight. So, I washed up, brushed my gap teeth, sucked on a Jolly Rancher to freshen my breath and went outside to join the others. Several smiled and shouted.

"There she is, we need you out here! Why didn't you want to come out?" So many questions all at the same time.

"I knew you guys were not going to let me sleep in peace. I don't know what I was thinking." I said jokingly.

As sleepy as I was and with so many thoughts racing through my mind I still found it within myself to make everyone around me have a much better day by telling them about my plans to celebrate my birthday on the 19th. I had talked Rea-Rea into doing a wet t-shirt show and Man-Man into dancing. She somewhat reminded me of the beautiful LisaRaye. I asked one of my two singers to sing "Happy Birthday" and the other to sing "Seems Like You Ready". The women sat around eagerly listening to the jailhouse promoter. "Well, Tippy's birthday is on the 23rd. I'm going to get a sock and tie her hands behind her back and let Rea-Rea dance for her. I'm going to order about fifteen honey buns and make a honey bun cake and order some tuna and tortillas and make some wraps. I will have a menu made up and it will be invitation only." I explained.

I had the women on the bottom level trying to move upstairs just to be out on activity time with me.   I pretty much stayed on clean-up and was able to be out with both most of the time.

They all talked about how they couldn't wait to enjoy the birthday celebrations.   Really deep down inside I knew I wasn't the only one who woke up feeling like giving up, but to be able to uplift someone else's spirit really made me feel better inside.

As I walked back inside after the hour went so quickly, Deputy Cole, asked me if I wanted to be on clean-up with three others.   Since I was already awake and didn't want to be locked in cell #221,   I answered.

"Yes, Deputy Cole, and thank you for asking."

She replied.   "Thank you!"

Deputy Cole was such a classy and clean woman.   She really believed in the following the guidelines as far as keeping the unit clean and smelling as fresh as possible.   She had us go room to room to clean as if we were working at a hotel.   The smell and odors of some of these women were just unbearable and would almost take the hair off of your head.   Once we got to the units in the back of the jail, I noticed an older woman in the lock-down area standing behind the door as the guard unlocked the middle door to slide the trays and cups inside to the inmates.   The inmate in cell# 113 looked as if she had been in jail her entire life.

She was in her late sixties, twigs all over her head, hazel eyes, 5'4", and weighed about 125 pounds.   She smiled at me as she stood there with a cup full of urine waiting on Sgt. Gib to come back there to get a taste of her bodily fluids.   She spoke to Deputy Cole who asked her nicely to pour the urine out.

"I had this for Sgt. Gib, but I will pour it out for you."   She said.

Afterwards she would make it her business to come by my cell during the one hour she was out for activity time to ask for a cigarette. I gave them to her cause I surely didn't want a warm splash of her sweet tea piss. Ugh!

After finishing clean-up I returned to cell# 221 after taking a hot shower and jumped up on the top bunk craving to write. It was finally the end of the first shift. In the midst of writing about thirty minutes later I heard again. "Standing head count." The "B" shift had arrived. I thought to myself I must go for lunch at chow-time to get a soy burger, beans, potato salad, and four cookies.
Happy Fourth of July to me…Ugh!

About an hour into writing a deputy on the "B" shift came and said. "Richardson, you are on clean-up." I walked downstairs to help get things started for the evening. I also made a few phone calls to some people on the outside that I really missed before going over to the ice maker to prepare for another round of dinner and light cleaning.

The good part about clean-up is that you are not locked down in your cell all day and are able to make phone calls. Plus, you are able to communicate with the other inmates on the top and bottom levels. I could also hear real coverage of the stories that made the top news in Little Rock, Arkansas.

News stories such as the Leah Monroe malicious arson cases. She was charged with burning down apartment buildings and other structures. Leah is a white female, 5'4", 165 lbs, grayish shoulder length hair, and a pretty smile. She told me how I made her wet her pants by laughing so hard. The laughter got me to the truth of these women stories. Something the Feds, media, detectives, attorneys, prosecutors, public defenders, psychologist, etc, couldn't get.

131

I tuned in with all smiles and listening ears to the stories of the untold truths as the ladies willing shared their stories with AngieSaidThat live at 3201 W. Roosevelt in Little Rock, Arkansas.

Leah walked over to me smiling after laughing at something I had said.   She sat down in front of me as I laid my head on Toe-Toe's leg while she oiled my scalp.   Leah and Toe-Toe shared cell# 108.

"Happy Fourth of July and how are you feeling today?"   I asked.

"Thanks Angie, I'm doing okay."   She answered.

Toe-Toe got straight to the point.   "Leah, tell Angie your story."   She said.

"Leah, I am writing a book and I would love to share your story in my book."   I said.

"Sure Angie, I will tell you the truth and you can ask me whatever you want to ask me.   I really enjoy talking to you and I think you are hilarious."   She said smiling.

Chapter 24

Leah Monroe,
Fire Starter
June 8, 2014

My name is Leah Monroe, I am Federal Inmate 17406-008 and I am in here for arson.   In October 2012, my beloved grandmother died. She wanted me there with her when she passed away, but because I did not get along with a certain cousin, I wasn't able to be there.   I fell into a deep depression and didn't want to be around my family and friends.   I had a friend that came to live with me during that time.   She began giving me Valium and Hydrocodone.   Her daughter would also come over and give me pills.   I was also taking Klonopin every day.   It numbed the pain, I felt nothing.   I was living in the South Building at Forest Place Apartments.   I had a beautiful apartment and I loved it.   I loved my neighbors so much, most were elderly and the community was more like a home than an apartment complex.

In December 2012, I had to move from the South Building to the North Building. I moved from a two bedroom to a one bedroom. I hated it. It was so small and my kids did not have their own bedroom anymore. I wasn't working and my family was tired of paying the expensive rent for the two bedrooms.

In January I started seeing Sean Howell. He was 38 years old and had been married three times. He was also severely depressed and emotionally and mentally abusive. By this time my pill habit was out of control. I was talking Xanax, Valium, Klonopin, Hydrocodone, Anatryptaline, and Soma's.

On February 24 & 25, 2013, I set two fires in the trash chute outside of my apartment. I got out of the bed in the middle of the night dressed in my pajamas and set my trash chute on fire and then return to bed. Although the relationship was awful, I continued to see Sean. By March, he had begun to cheat on me and to say cruel things to me. I do not believe I set any fires in March or April. I cannot remember. In May I discovered that he had multiply girlfriends and that I had contracted a venereal disease. I went home on May 16th, and took an Ambien and one of each of the other pills that I was addicted to at this point. I also drank a six pack of Mike's Ice. At some point that night I got up and lit a fire in the trash chute that ultimately burned the building down. I remember bits and pieces of that night. It comes to me in flashbacks and a lot when I am sleeping. My neighbor upstairs eyes were swollen shut from the smoke. A little girl was screaming, "Daddy, daddy!" And an elderly lady was rescued from the balcony of her third floor apartment by the fire department.

I went home with my mom that night. I don't remember calling her. It seems as if she just appeared there. The building was totally destroyed and I lost everything I had. I did not have insurance. I moved in with my parents, but I would go to my ex-husband's house everyday to keep the children since they were out of school for the summer. I was taking the prescription pills every day.

Sometime in June, my ex-husband and the kids went out of town and I was house-sitting. At some point I got up again in the middle of the night, went to the storage room off the carport, got several flammable substances, drove back to Forest Place Apartments and lit an elevator on fire. I have no memory of it whatsoever, but my ex-husband identified the evidence left behind as items missing from the storage room of his home. The fire was a pretty bad one and a fireman dislocated his shoulder that night.

The ATF (Arkansas Tobacco & Firearm) and Arkansas State Police came to my ex-husband's home at some point to interview me. They were interviewing everyone that lived in the apartments. It was something about that interview that made me a suspect, perhaps my body language or something I said. I was still strung out on those pills and there is no telling what I said. However, even after that interview, I went back to Forest Place Apartments in the middle of the night and set a fire in the hallway outside of someone's door. There were children in that apartment. A pregnant woman had to jump off of her balcony. This really devastated me because I would never consciously hurt another human being. Several times during the month of June, while I was living at my parent's house, I was getting up in the middle of the night and driving back to Forest Place Apartments and setting fires. I would return back to the house and go back to sleep with all my clothes and even my shoes on. Why? I have no idea. I have never committed a crime in my life. I have never even had a speeding ticket.

During this time, of course the apartment fires were all over the news and all over a Facebook page called *Forbidden Hillcrest*. I was a member on this particular page also. I started commenting on the posts, saying things like, "Only 10% of arsonist ever get caught", and other comments I don't even remember. The ATF have copies of all of them.

On July 3, 2013, the ATF and the Arkansas State Police called me and said that they needed me to come and look at mug shots. That's what they said, however when I got there an officer with the ATF and a State Police Officer met me at the door and escorted me to a back office.   When I sat down, one of the officers slid a   piece of paper out from under a file and asked me if I knew someone name Michael.

"No" I answered.

He asked me if I thought he was stupid.

"No" I again answered.

He said, "You called me stupid on Facebook."

I took my phone out to see what he was talking about and he snatched it from my hand.   I tried to get it back and he said, "No."   He stated that if I sign something giving him permission to look in my phone that he would download the information and return it right back to me. So I did.   He walked down the hall and then said I could get it back in three days.

"You can't trick me like that!"   I said.

"I am a Federal Agent and I can do whatever I want."   He said and I quote.

He brought my phone back to my ex-husband's house on Friday, July 5th.   On July 6, 2013, I went to Pinnacle Mountain and took an overdose of Prozac and Lamictal, my two psychiatric medications that I was also taking.   The park ranger found me in my SUV and called a State Trooper.   I was given a DUI and taken by ambulance to Baptist Hospital.   I was there a week and my vehicle was impounded.   My mom came and got me and took me home to her house.   After that I stopped taking the Xanax, Valium, and all the other pills that were not mine.   I was back in my right head.   There were no more fires or anything at all after that.

In September 2013, the Feds subpoenaed my dad to a grand jury. He identified his gas can as being one that was used to set one of the fires. He came out of the grand jury room crying and told my mom that they were going to arrest me. I had been put on Lithium shortly after the July suicide attempt. I tried to commit suicide again that night on the Lithium because I knew I had hurt a lot of people and know my parents were being hurt too. I ended up at UAMS Psychiatric Research Institute for a week. They changed my medication and I felt better than I had felt in my life. Everything was quiet.

On February 9, 2014, my children came to my mom's house to play in the snow. They wanted me to build a snowman with them. I said no because I was cold natured and being outside was miserable to me. I was also very, very lazy. My mom went outside and built a snowman with my two daughters, aged 6 and 7. The next morning at 8:30 AM, I went into the kitchen to get coffee and I saw a man run down the side yard right through my mom's flower bed. I looked out and saw the ATF, the Arkansas State Police, and the Little Rock Police. There were cars, trucks, and suburbans all over the front of the house and all down the side street of my parent's house. They rang the doorbell and I opened the door. About 10 – 12 agents with bullet proof vests and guns came rushing through the front door. They grabbed me and sat me on the hearth of the fireplace. They were all screaming at once, "Where is everybody? Who all is in the house?" Four agents rushed down the hall and marched my 65 year old father out of his office and pushed him down on an ottoman and all four stood over him.

My mom asked, "What are you doing? We are not criminals."

The ATF officer said, "No, but she is going to jail and if you don't shut your mouth, you are going with her. I am not going to listen to any of your shit."

I was handcuffed and led out of the front door passed my little girls' snowman and into a police car. They took me to Pulaski County Jail.

February 9th, was the last time I saw my children and February 10th was the last time I saw my parents.

Leah eventually accepted a plea deal and was sentenced to twelve years in the Federal Prison.   She destroyed millions of dollars in commercial property and placed numerous of people lives in danger and yet she is sentenced to only twelve years.

Why have I been so unfairly sentenced when I have no prior convictions, have never owned a gun and have never been seen with a gun?

Where is the justice for AngieSaidThat?

Chapter 25

Prisoner of Hope

This devotional is dedicated to Christian friends who are incarcerated, some for long periods of time. Please know that you have a role model to follow in the story of Joseph as found in the book of Genesis, Chapters 37 – 42. GOD has a purpose for you to fulfill wherever you are, regardless of how, why, or when you got there, or how long you need to stay.

Even if we are not physically confined, we can find ourselves in prisons of doubt, hopelessness, carnal living, or false religion. Every prison, whether physical or otherwise, hold the possibility of hope if we take our eyes off the walls and turn them to GOD.

As our congregation ministers to inmates in a nearby prison, I am impressed with the testimonies we hear. Some have told us that incarceration was just what they needed to stop them of their ungodly living and to help them find the Lord. We seek to encourage those who seek working in this way.

Consider how useful Joseph was in spite of his unjust imprisonment. His character was so upright and his life was so faithful that even as a prisoner he ruled the prison! His focus was not on himself but on others. He reached out to give help and hope where he could. His long years in prison were his training school for great and useful to many people after his release.

What are your opportunities? If you feel that you have none and you meet each day with despair, it is time to take your eyes off the walls around you.

Look to GOD, the stronghold of today's key verse. He has a person for you now. Look about you and find opportunities to encourage others and point them to GOD. He has a double blessing for you to serve your fellow man with hope.

What lies behind us and what lies before us are tiny matters...compared to what lies within us.
Ralph Waldo Emerson

Chapter 26

Prisoner of the State
July 16, 2014

Three days before my 44th birthday, I was awaken by a guard at 3201 W. Roosevelt.   She thought I was asleep as she looked through the cell door, but saw that I was up with my paper and pencil writing. Earlier Tuesday night I couldn't understand why I didn't receive any of the commissary I had order.   I did get the I-Care package from My Wife that contained an assortment of candy bars.   As always most of the guards don't know the answers to any of the commissary questions.   It's never their jobs.   A few minutes later another inmate named Amanda came to the door and said, "Some people are zero'd out, which means they are on their way to prison."   I looked over at my cellmate.   We both felt some type of way.   My comedic personality had touched so many people in such a short period of time.   I had asked my attorney friend, Stanley, to get me moved to Newport Prison, but I didn't expect it to be so soon.

I felt it all over my body.   This was the reason I had not received my commissary.   I looked at all my favorite candy bars from My Wife and wondered was this a special way of saying good-bye without either one of us knowing it.

Bye-bye! I was on my way to prison in Newport, Arkansas.

I rushed to the telephone to call my sister, Sharon.

"Doll Baby, listen I just found out that I am leaving going to prison in the morning. I can't talk long, plus I don't have much time to be out. I will call you when I get there and get situated, okay?" I spoke softly swallowing my tears. I didn't want her to know my eyes had formed with tears.

"Nooo!" she screamed and started crying. "Sister, are you serious? So soon, already?" she asked.

"Yes, Doll Baby, get yourself together for me. I need you to be strong because I am. Trust me. I'm going to be home sooner than you think even with this hurricane verdict. I promise." I spoke clearly trying to uplift her spirits.

"Okay, I love you," she said crying.

"Bye and I love you too, Doll Baby" I replied and hung of the phone to call My Wife.

"Hey Baby, I'm leaving in the morning. I'm zero'd out." I told her.

She spoke very softly and clear, "Are you for real, you leaving already? I won't be able to see you this Sunday?" She asked.

"No, Baby, please don't sound like that, okay? I'm going to write and call you the first time I get a chance too. You know it will be two weeks or so. I'm not sure how it works, but just pray and stay strong. I don't have much time out, but trust me, I am going to write you soon. I can't take anything with me but my Bible. I got time to take a shower and that's it. Baby, I miss you and I love you through it all." I spoke with sincerity.

"I love you too and I am going to be strong. I am not going to give up on you" she assured me.

"Promise?" I asked.

"I promise." she answered.

I felt some type of way after those two phone calls. I also called my friend, Tweedy, who has shown so much love and support. I can't thank GOD enough for her and a few others. I realized that it is in times like this and other difficult situations that reveal those who really care about you. It is times like this that reveals those who believe in you and know that you are a fighter too, even during the worst of times. It also reveals those that are haters. Most will not even write or send you a dime, but will be gossiping about the bad situation you are in to anyone that will entertain them or that Facebook garbage. They will pretend to care. Just fake!

To hear the outcome of the unfair justice and the amount of time given, some may think I will never return again. But to return with more power than before and in Jesus name! And a comeback with a purpose! Unstoppable! Who do you know has this type of faith, but AngieSaidThat?

I jumped in the shower as Hot Pepper and KT sat at the table waiting for me to finish. I spent my last ten minutes of activity time saying good-bye to all the other inmates. I walked outside with the two of them and shouted, "All of y'all may as well go on suicide watch because there will be no more comedy. I am leaving!" I did a little booty dance for one of the inmates 21st birthday and cracked everyone up. We all laughed and hugged. Before I knew it I heard,

"Ladies time to lock it down", one of the guards shouted as I was trying to throw my ass in a circle. UGH!

I could tell by the look in KT's eyes that she wanted to leave with me. She was only twenty years old and sentenced to 25 years on a "Y" felony, which means she will have to serve 70% before she is eligible for parole. She walked up to me with a bad limp in her walk and asked me to write her and if I could get her moved. She also said how she wanted to be with me on that bus to prison. I had enjoyed mentoring her and several others at 3201 W. Roosevelt. Overall they had listened to me and seemed to have enjoyed it as well. Hot Pepper didn't try to hold back what and how she felt. She had developed feelings for me through me making her laugh and the positive words I shared with her. I made it clear to her and all the others about my girlfriend and many respected my relationship. Truth be told, I am a flirt and have made mistakes in my past that have caused trust issues, but I am only human and I learned from those mistakes.

I stood at Hot Pepper's cell door and talked to her about staying in touch even though she had to appear in court in a few weeks to be sentenced to Federal time. There were a few people that I wanted to stay in contact with that I had discussed business ideas with and I wanted to keep encouraging them to stay on the right track in life. I knew without a doubt I would keep mentoring the younger LGBT generation. The fact of who I am and to be living the life of a prisoner. Who can tell it better than I can? Nobody!

I hugged Hot Pepper and headed back to cell# 206. To my surprise I was moved into cell# 206 with Tippy. We became extremely close. She opened up to me about her entire childhood life and how she felt about her murder charge. We talked about it all, but due to the fact that she has not gone to trial yet, I cannot and will not go into detail about what no one knows but her, the deceased boyfriend, and GOD. Tippy looked up at me as I walked into cell# 206.

"So you know I am really going to miss you? I've been here over eight months and no one has ever made me laugh or open up and talk about my life or the things I have gone through. Angie, with your personality and your compassion for understanding, you make it so easy for people to open up to you. I know this place is not going to be the same without you and I can't wait to read your book." She said.

"Tippy, listen I know you like me as more than just friends and you know how I feel about my lover. Just know if she wasn't in my life that maybe things could have been on another level since I know you are coming to Newport too. But I love her and I will never again make her feel the way I did once in the past, no matter if I am inside or outside of these bars. I don't ever want you to think that you are not beautiful, because you are Tippy. People in your past may have put you down and you have carried that with you all of your life. It has affected your self esteem so much that you believe it. Pray for change and prepare yourself for whatever you have to face. People will always judge us, crime or no crime, prisoner or no prisoner. It's time to believe that GOD will make unbelievable movements, know that HE can move mountains. I know your story and I believe it was a mistake. You know three minutes of anger or the wrong decision can cause anyone to be in one of these dusty blue uniforms. GOD still loves you through it all. I am going to stay in contact with you. I want you to get the Act 3 hold lifted off of you and bail out of here and spend time with your girls." I said to her with a serious look on my face.

"Angie, that's all I want to do. I know that I am going to have to do some time and I should be punished. I'm the reason why my boyfriend is dead. My girls know that I did something wrong at the ages of five and seven. Saturday during visitation my five year old asked me, Mama will they let you out for your birthday next week if you are good?" She spoke with tears forming in her eyes that she couldn't hold back. She cried and cried.

"Well they don't understand the law, hell even at my age I don't understand some of these sentences, but you will be able to touch and hold them at Newport. All of this is hard, but soon you will be able to turn those tears into a beautiful smile with laughter and meaning. You remember the first time I let you oil my hair? All I thought about was the fact that those were the same hands you used to stab him with that night.

I'm very well known and have helped many people, but who am I to judge anyone? People are going to judge us no matter what. Just get your mind ready for all the talking. I couldn't have chosen a better cellmate. Didn't I tell you I was going to get moved into this cell? I don't regret the move. I am thankful to have been able to uplift your spirit. I am truly going to miss you and this cell will never be the same." We both laughed.

She looked at me and said, "Well Bissh, fix my last super!" We high-fived one another and laughed out loud again.

During the short period of time I was in cell# 206, Tippy and I became really close. People questioned her as to whether we had anything going on, but my mind wasn't on any of that sex behind the bars mess. I enjoyed writing and she enjoyed reading, she graduated with honors. I couldn't spell most of my words, but she became my jailhouse Google and dictionary and I became her giggle. I enjoyed making up dishes out of the commissary items we ordered. I have always been creative. We shared items so that we both could save more of the money that was put on our books. She also had to face the same judge that had unfairly sentenced me. Due to the fact of me knowing the possible outcome of a jury trial with ineffective counsel and the unfair sentence it had gotten me, I tried to talk her out of a jury trial after listening to the circumstance of her crime, but the decision is ultimately hers. We both agreed on how unfair it was that an inmate with prior convictions and facing eight aggravated robberies only got twenty-five years and me a first timer with no convictions got twenty-one years.   Is this justice served fairly?   I don't think so!

One of my favorite daily scriptures as I walk this path is and continue to appeal this nightmare for justice is Psalm 58;

Do you judge uprightly?   Do you rulers know the meaning of the word? Do you judge the people fairly? You hand out violence instead of justice.   No matter how skillfully they play, they spit poison like deadly snakes, ignoring the tunes of the snake charmer.   Oh, GOD, speak to my heart.   I need your guidance.

If the Bible speaks on it, I am okay with the appeals if the right people are in the right place.   It's funny how Judge Pecker, who is now an attorney due to his own run-in with the law, represented Marty, my co-defendant.   Pecker knew the truth about Marty's boyfriend really being the one dressed in the wig and who has a gap in his teeth larger than mine.   So, yes the case was flipped on me and he also knew I had been acquitted years ago because he was the judge on my case in 2003. Is that not a conflict of interest?   Is this really how the law works?   Is it fair that I should be serving twenty-one years on a "Y",   meaning I have to serve 70% before I am eligible for parole, but his client had his charges dropped to simple robbery although he has three prior gun charges and is currently on probation.   Was justice truly served?

Chapter 27

Newport Prison

Tippy and I talked and laughed until about 11:30 PM after I made her last supper. I picked up my paper and pencil and wrote a letter to KT. The special rush and feelings I get while writing is something I can't explain. It felt better than any seven or eleven on the dice table. It felt better than any cocaine addiction, crack, meth, pills, sex or any other addiction. I'm addicted to writing. Before I knew it the guard was knocking and screaming, "Richardson, wake up and pack." I was never asleep. I usually wrote all night until morning. GOD allowed me to feed my spirit by writing versus being irritated over commissary. I believe it and I receive it!

I gave out a few candy bars and left everything else with Tippy. She loves chocolate. I enclosed all my writings inside three large envelopes as Tippy woke up to help me pack. I rushed to mail off the most important possessions of my life, my new found purpose in life. I mailed them to my good friend, Kim, with instructions on what to do until I got situated in prison. I continued rushing to get everything else together as the guard repeatedly called my name to report downstairs. I looked at the clock after hugging Tippy good-bye. It was 3:35 AM. As I walked from cell# 206, I walked past cell# 201 and Hot Pepper was standing in the door window.

"Why are you awake this early?" I asked.

"I knew you would be leaving. I am going to miss you, really." She spoke with her Spanish accent. "I'm going to be sad without you here."

I noticed the other Mexicans in the doors screaming, "Good-bye Lesbiana." I laughed as I walked down the stairs and assuring Hot Pepper that we would stay in touch. When I got downstairs all the inmates were up as if no one had gone to sleep. Some cried. I hugged them as I held back my tears knowing that I had left a special mark and impression at 3201 W. Roosevelt. I will continue to pray for improvements of conditions for the inmates as well as the staff. That place is horrible! There is no other word for it.

I walked into the holding room with five other inmates waiting to get on the bus to be driven to prison. My mind raced in so many different places. My heart ached from the phone calls. My stomach was weak thinking about it all. Who am I to turn to? I rushed back upstairs asking the nice guard on duty to please open the door to cell# 206 so that I could get my Bible. I didn't care about anything else on the road trip. I couldn't have made it without my Bible.

Another guard came to get us and took us to another musty, nasty, pissy smelling holding cell at 3201 W. Roosevelt. The conditions are sickening, infected with germs and need to be inspected. People complain but never do anything about it. I left too soon, but numerous inmates wrote letters to me about the mold, dust, and germs. No one deserves to be in these kind of conditions or treatment. Not the inmates or the employees. A Hot mess!

AngieSaidThat

A few women from Unit A joined us. We were all dressed in the street clothes we wore in before the dusty blues. About twelve of us were crowded into a small holding cell. From the smell of things maybe only two of us bothered to shower. At that moment not only was my freedom being robbed of me, I also felt like my ears, nose and throat were stuffed with the body parts of animals. The odor was a charge within itself. Attempted murder at 3201 W. Roosevelt. I thought I was going to die.

They served us breakfast. The other ladies rushed out of the cell to those cold pancakes like we had been dropped off at the nearest I-Hop. I sat against the wall on the concrete bench closest to the door trying to get past the odors. We sat in the room for hours waiting to load up on the bus. I watched the men walk by looking in the cell and asking the women to flash them. I am gay true enough, but the smell puzzled me. Totally disrespectful to any woman, lesbian or not!

All I could hear or see was people chained around their waist, ankles, and hands. I thought about last Thanksgiving when the movie *"Roots"* played on the television all day. My mind raced over and over at the loss of my freedom and how I got railroaded. As I was in deep thoughts the door opened. A guard stood in the door with a list calling our names to be handcuffed. I was chained to three other women. I'm so glad they did not chain us around our waist and ankles.

Mrs. Jamison and Melvina walked us to the new fresh smelling van. Yeah, riding in style, but the jailhouse living conditions are pitiful. As I looked out the window at the familiar streets that I once traveled freely every day, I tried to ease my mind and talk to the other inmates. I couldn't believe I was on my way to prison with them. Two of the white women assured me that my name was well-known.
"Everybody knows AngieSaidThat or of Angie, the only black gay club owner in Little Rock." They said.

The guard turned tuned the radio to 106.3 and at that moment my mind and memory got the best of me. A song by Brian McKnight, titled

"Anything" was playing. It instantly reminded me of my club at 3910 and the time I lip-synced it myself. My heart replayed memories of my family, relationships, and my life in general. I found myself snapping my fingers and then quickly snapping myself back into the reality that I was on a ride to prison as I looked down at my handcuffed hands. I went from singing to crying. The cries I had been holding back. The cry that my friend, Kim, had asked if I had allowed myself. She said don't try to hold it in, just have a good cry and let it out. I covered my face with the white jacket of pants suit.

The white girl sitting next to me said, "I don't cry too quickly, but you have touched me." She touched my leg, but I never uncovered my face on the ride to prison. I really needed to get that out of me. With about ten minutes away from the prison my mind was ready to face the punishment. It wasn't the punishment that I couldn't bear, it was the ineffective counseling, the conflict of interest, and the unfair sentencing that got the best of me. Unjustified!

We arrived about 10:00 AM. The gates were like I have seen in prison movies. I was about to enter them myself. A bunch of women from different counties were being dropped off as well. All I saw was guards and many inmates in white uniforms. Time we walked inside the gate they removed the handcuffs and a guard was screaming and ordered us to stand in a single line. The intake process took about three hours. It had to be about fifty women or more. Everyone walked out of a room in a white gown. It looked like two sheets that were sewn together. I noticed something that looked like perm in everyone's hair. I knew I was really on my way as the line moved forward into that same room and I would be dressed in a white gown and that stuff placed into my hair. I asked one of the other inmates in line what was that stuff they were putting into our heads. She explained to me it was to keep everyone from getting head lice. They applied it like my old hairstylist use to do when he was giving me a fresh perm. I would have much rather been in a salon versus behind these gates getting a lice treatment.

"Richardson, what size shoes, underwear, bra, pants and shirt do you wear?" An inmate by the last name of Robertson asked. I later found out she had been there for fifteen years and this was her job at the prison. I walked inside the door and the guard asked.

"Do you want to donate your clothes or send them home?"

"Throw them away. I don't want any memories of that day." I answered and signed off on the paperwork for my clothes and shoes.

"Take this bag in the room behind you and place everything in it." She said as she escorted me into the room and watched me get undressed. "Open your mouth and move your tongue up and down. I need you to spread your legs apart and squat and cough." She spoke firmly and with authority.

I proceeded as ordered and coughed.

"No, cough harder and open up." She demanded.

I coughed even harder thinking this can't be happening to me.

"Now turn around and spread your butt cheeks apart and cough again." She ordered. "Bend over, spread your vagina, and cough. Open it up and cough. Cough again." She ordered.

I coughed and at that moment I felt beneath the ants. I can't even explain the feeling of that process. I was thankful that I didn't eat breakfast that morning. A coughing mess! She was looking for tobacco or other substances. I almost delivered a bowel movement if I would of had to cough just one more cough. I put on my white sheet and a pair of no name cheap shoes. Inmate Robertson was waiting and ready to put that lice cream in my hair. She placed a double squeeze amount in my hands to place under my armpits and on my private parts that were now exposed to Newport Prison with hard double cough and no longer private.

After about six more had been processed in we formed a line and walked to another area and had to shower in front of each other with a half of a bath towel. Once I showered I had to stand naked waiting on my all white uniform, a white bra, white panties, socks, pants, and shirt with your ADC booking number and name attached.

You are not allowed to use the restroom during the entire time this is taking place. Before we were able to take a shower, we had to fill out paperwork listing an emergency contact, answering if you wanted to be buried or cremated, picture taken for your ID badge, and fingerprinted. Too many questions and answers in this room with over fifty women waiting. We all had bags in the hallway that contained three pair of panties, three pairs of socks, three rolls of toilet tissue, one razor, one bar of soap, a toothbrush broken in half, a set of thermal underwear, a pair of old boots, and a thick winter jacket. There were also two white sheets, two blankets, a robe, one pillow case and thirty maxi pads with wings. I believe I can fly! I wished I could fly up out of here!

My head was aching. I had been up all night the night before writing with a purpose. I hadn't eaten or drank anything and I had just coughed myself dry. The process was taking forever and I just wanted to lay down. We had to pick up both our bags and walk and stay behind the yellow line. I walked into Medical and recognized one of the nurses that had been to my club. She could not believe I was sitting there in an all white prison uniform. We talked briefly as I answered questions about my medical history, but I was exhausted.

July 16th, changed my entire life on this first day of facing twenty-one years in prison. I prayed for healing to cure my headache. I felt so empty going through a light withdrawal of not being able to write and with nothing to write with. Tears formed in my eyes over needing and wanting my writing supplies.

I finally was able to get into bed several hours later. I laid with the Bible on my chest opened to Psalm 58 and thought about it all over again. Tears started rolling from my eyes again. I picked up my Bible and started reading Psalm 23. The Lord Is My Shepherd. I cried and I prayed until I drifted off to sleep to rest up to challenge the following day on finding out about the Law Library and understanding the rules and process to file an appeal for equality of justice.

AngieSaidThat

Chapter 28

Annette

The following morning I had no clue what time it was. I was awaken by a loud female voice screaming, "Chow, chow, chow, get up if you want to eat." I didn't move or open my eyes. I kept my eyes closed and prayed. I gave a special thanks to GOD that my monthly cycle had held back for hours. True enough Eve had eaten the forbidden fruit, but I'm so thankful that GOD hadn't placed a time limit on it. The thought of coughing while on my menstrual cycle is really unbearable.

I laid on the top bunk and felt the aching in my body. I missed so many people. The fact that I wasn't able to call or write anyone and that I had nothing to write with was like death row to me. I couldn't call on anyone but Jesus to hear to my cry. Jesus!

It took me back to 3201 W. Roosevelt on a Friday night at Bible Study with Annette. I will never forget how she shared her story of a sex addiction that started at the age of five. A babysitter molested her and her siblings. By the time she reached the sixth grade she had had several sexual encounters with several different boys and few with some older girls. She couldn't say no to anyone. She explained how she enjoyed it and started being the aggressor pursuing many boys. She felt as if she had to have it and needed it every day more times than what was normal, (whatever was normal to her.) She later started dating older men and selling herself for money in her early teenage years. Later on she was ganged raped. She had agreed to have sex with two of the people, but eight men raped her. Who would believe her? She enjoyed having sex and was known for her sex addiction. She continued to sell her body for years. She had her first son in the twelfth grade. She managed to stay in school and proudly took care of her son. She continued selling her body to older men. It was her job and the craving of her addiction. Because of it all, she decided to move from her neighborhood to the other side of town to clean up her act and hoping no one would know about her means of making money. She met a truck driver, what woman doesn't want a truck driver? That is also one of the hottest spot to get paying customers. She explained how she met a special man. They dated, but she was qualified to be his wife. The relationship didn't last very long. Years later she finally got married and had one more child. She wanted to change her life, but the sex addiction over powered her. It wasn't long before her marriage became emotionally, physically, and mentally abusive. He called her many whores, not knowing her past history and how it affected her knowing the deep secrets within her heart. She later moved to Houston, Texas, with him. As she spoke I started writing with my purpose and listening closely to her.

"My pastor enjoys this part of my story. My husband and I were on the way to Houston. We got into a pretty bad argument. He hit me as we argued even while he was driving. He talked to me so bad, calling me many names. I couldn't stand it anymore. He couldn't pull over in the middle of the speeding traffic, so I crawled into the back seat and took my shoes off. All I could think about was us dying, but I didn't care. I started just beating him from the back seat. It wasn't anything he could do. He pulled over on the exit and dragged me out of the car and beat me really badly and left me there. All I could do was pray to GOD to give me the strength to make it back to the highway. I only knew my way to my sister's house from the highway. I didn't care how long it would take me, but I knew I was going to make it there. He left me in my truck!" She explained.

I thought to myself, "What's Love Got To Do With It?"

Once I got to my sister's house, I explained to her what had happened. I called him and demanded my truck back. The following day he picked me up as if nothing had ever happened." She continued. "A few days later I left him and half way out of Houston I turned around to go back and get him. I wasn't ready to leave him. I wanted my marriage to work." She further explained. "The fighting continued and this last time I returned to Little Rock and packed. I couldn't move to Houston with him. I cried and cried and called out loud to Jesus. I repeated Jesus, Jesus, Jesus! I looked for him under my bed, I looked for him in the closet. I called his name over and over. He heard my cry. He gave me the strength to leave him. So, here I am. I started to sell my body again to pay bills and provide for my children. I didn't do it as much, but I had to pay my bills. Older men will pay."

I looked at her. The inmates noticed and said, "Angie is writing." We all laughed as I continued looking at her and deeply listening.

"Do you mind if I share your story? I am writing a book and would love to share this testimony about how GOD changed you and cured your sex addiction." I asked.

She smiled and said, "Sure, I knew my name and story would become famous." She laughed and so did the rest of us.

She continued talking and ended with a very special prayer calling on Jesus. She gave me chills. I pulled out a blank page from the New Testament with Psalms and Proverbs. I wrote her a small note to show my appreciation for her coming to 3201 W. Roosevelt and sharing her amazing story with us. She is a very powerful woman and GOD has his favor on her. I encouraged her to keep the notes because my book was going to move mountains. I looked forward to another Bible Study with her, but now I am at Newport.

Annette really did something to me that made me insert her inside my memory box. I couldn't bring my notes that I had quickly written down. I do know she attends a Pentecostal Church in Mayflower, AR. She is brown-skinned, 5'4", 155 lbs, short brownish blond hair, brown

eyes, a pretty smile and nice looking. She reminds me of my half-sister on my dad's side. Their voices sounded alike and they had similar ways. I missed the closeness I once had with my half-sister, but how do people mend a broken heart, even with family?

Now that I am currently sitting in Newport, I soul search a lot within myself. The moment the guard told us that we would get $12.00 from the Newport Prison Compound on our second day to shop. We got to order off the indignant list. I didn't care about anything on the limited list, but I wanted to know if writing pads, pens, pencils, envelopes, and stamps were on the list. I prayed and surely enough those items were listed and now I am writing with it. I couldn't wait to return to cell# 213 to write My Wife, my sisters, Tweedy, and Keacia to send my prayers for her Mama who meant so much to me. I remembered their addresses in my head. For those that I couldn't remember I enclosed their letters inside another to get my message out. I used four of the six envelopes within two hours. I knew it would be another week before I could shop with my own money and have a larger variety of things to choose from.

I jumped into the shower after waiting almost an hour for fifty-four women that stood before me or after me. We all wanted to shower. So many people spent five dollars and some change on shower shoes. Baby, my toes could have peeled like a new born baby's booty, because I had to write! I didn't sit around as the others did to watch television and talk. I walked into cell# 213 with the best feeling.

The feeling of relief to have my writing supplies helped me to rest better. My tears dried away, but probably until my first visit. It's not so much the sadness of my first visit from My Wife, because I am so thankful to have her by my side, unless she leaves me. The thought of seeing her smile again was priceless. I needed my heart to beat again. I needed to share my experiences to make her laugh versus making her cry. I knew exactly how to turn the most emotional moments into much needed laughter.

I soon got sick of hearing inmates sentencing stories and how much time they were sentenced to. I felt like I should have been in the next room with a small hallway and glass doors between us. A guard was sitting and looking like he was watching a Death Row monitor. I even observed the patients in their cells after certain medical problems restricted them from immediate family. The medical administration had to approve all visits for inmates who are in the hospital for an extended length of time, more than 7 – 10 days, or in case of terminal illness or critical condition. Same place visits are approved that can exceed the four hour visit. I read and made sure to continue reading all the different rules that are in place here at the Arkansas Department of Correction. I haven't been here a week yet, and this is already a story in the prison life of AngieSaidThat.

I walked into the gym for activity time to be observant and check it out. Some of the other inmates asked me if I had been here before. They said my name was well-known even before I arrived and could get myself together. I got more messages than the mail room damn near from people I had no clue about in one day. I really got respect from the LGBT community. Some of the women that worked in the kitchen passed me messages. I was told my smile was going to get me in a lot of trouble. Well, it truly got me convicted wrongfully.

One of the studs walked up to me in the gym. I knew Ke-Ke from my club. She was in the middle of a basketball game.

"Hey Bro, you good? I really didn't believe what I heard about your charge. There are different programs you can enroll in to get a job or even boot camp. Let me know if you need anything." She said.

"Hey, Lil Bro, thank you so much. I really appreciate the love Bro. So when are you leaving this place? When you finish come holler at me. I am going to sit down." I replied standing by the basketball goal.

"Okay Bro, I'm supposed to be out of here in March, but my class has dropped. I got to get my class back. These women will keep you here, Bro. I'm currently with this white girl in her name Mindy. She said that you know her and she has been to your club several times. Bro, these females in here hating and got us separated into different units." She explained.

"Well, Lil Bro, this is my second day here, and the last thing on my mind is these females. I'm sure I haven't seen everyone, but I am cool without the drama. I got to get my appeals going and stay in my lane. You feel me? I operated a gay club and I feel you on messy people." I said. "Come holler at me when you finish and again, thank you, Bro!" I smiled and walked to sit down.

"You good, Bro?" She asked.

I sat down on the bench and watched the inmates play volleyball and basketball. Some walked around the gym, some exercised, and some socialized. A few other studs walked over asking if I was okay. A few minutes later a female sat next to me.

"Hey, I like your hair. So, you are Angie? Um, you need to see me in my make-up." She said smiling.

I'm thinking to myself, is this a pick-up line? What, so soon! I noticed women looking at me, which wasn't surprising, but make-up, really? My thought within seconds of her mentioning her make-up was

Bitch, I'm facing twenty-one years and you think I give a damn about some eye-shadow, lipstick, or whatever the hell make-up you talking about! Are you kidding me? (In Frank's voice, the owner of Jazzi's), Commissary make-up, bitch please!

I looked at her and politely said, "I'm going to walk around for a minute."

She smiled and said, "Okay, talk to you later."

I'm thinking bullshit! I want no part of you and your Cover Girl make-up, Boo-Boo. UGH!

I noticed the women trying to be flirty and even doing chow the women at the next table were saying, "I want the blood head, she hasn't been here good yet and she is all the big talk. She's sexy."

Some of the inmates got messages to me real quick. I thanked those that told me about the special messages on my *AngieSaidThat* Facebook page. In just two days the respect played a major role, but I had to stay focused. The inmates that were processed in with me started making comments like, "Is that Angie with the gay club? We gonna walk to the chow-hall with you. I am going to say that I am your girlfriend." A few of them laughed. I smiled more so than ever, but my personality usually charmed many with laughter. It's just a natural ability I have. My Creator blessed me with a very special gift.

Chapter 29

Happy Birthday!
  July 19, 2014

*H*appy Birthday to me!   I woke up praying quickly to myself.
My mind thought about all the many people that wouldn't be celebrating
Little Rock Black Gay Pride and my birthday as well.   I knew that Little
Rock was not going to be the same without me around.   I targeted an
entire Gay community.   So many were missed, but the majority of them
weren't even a thought to me.   I know that some truly envied me
because of who I am and my accomplishments.   Some wanted to be in
my shoes.   Now they will be able to walk in a pair, but will they be able
to fill them?   Hell no!   I remember one in particular stud name KO
Dior.   Even in the midst of my storm and my spiritual healing and
changing heart, I liked nothing about her.   She's truly a snake and
should have been in court like Jo-Jo and the police impersonator, Fink,
showering evilness over me.   My heart is filled
with the spirit of love, but in reality some people hate you for what you
have accomplished.   They want to do what you are doing.   We are
all individuals with our own talents and gifts.   Instead of hating on
someone else for what they were blessed with, haters should find their

own passion and purpose and develop it. People may see a lot of gays, but that does not mean we are all on the same level of thinking. All attorneys don't represent the same. All the sport players don't play the same. People are pure haters, but admire me at the same time!

Today is my 44th birthday and I am sitting here at Newport Prison in all white versus in rainbow colors celebrating unity, pride and history. I still woke up thanking GOD and celebrating my purpose of writing, making these ladies laugh, and overall the power of planning a comeback. I wasn't able to make phone calls, but my spirit has touched those close to me. I mailed out letters and I was down to one envelope until Thursday, and today is only Saturday. Wow!

I went to the gym and worked out on the light equipment in here and then back to my cell to continue writing until the showers were opened and available. I noticed the other inmates watching television and talking. We had eaten earlier. The menu consisted of cornbread, spinach, watermelon, mashed potatoes, and beef hamburger patties. I ate the spinach, watermelon, and cornbread. I didn't attend breakfast and I'm not ever planning on it, but facing so much time that is subject to change. I do know I want to remain healthy in this place and the thick beef they serve in here is not on my to do list. I thought about becoming a veggie lover. Now I understand why so many inmates released from this place gain a lot of weight. I noticed in the gym the items listed on the commissary list would be more of my eating choices.

I looked over in cell# 114 and listened to another inmate speaking about a Mrs. Ritter, who once lived in that same cell for over ten years waiting to be put to sleep. She was on death row for killing her two children. She was formerly a nurse and tried to kill herself but failed. She injected needles into her kids and the burning sensation caused one of them to cry out in pain, she then picked up a pillow and placed it over his face until he stopped breathing. I walked to the doorway of the cell and chills covered my body instantly knowing she was once here. She was put to sleep by lethal injections in 2011 at Cummins Prison Farm.

The thought of me watching prisoner movies and reading prisoner stories and now writing my own from personal experience was just amazing to me. To see everyone dressed in the same attire and limited time of fifteen minutes or less to eat in chow-hall was something serious and unbelievable.

I finally started talking to some of the other inmates about the horrific squat and cough ordeal. Open it up, turn around, cough harder, bend over, and throw it in every mathematical form of a square, triangle, rectangle and finally a circle. UGH! Inmate Anya, who is 5'3", 165 lbs, dark skinned, short nappy hair, brown eyes, walked with a physical disability. She struggled with drug addiction problems as well.

She stood from sitting on the stairs and said, "Yeah, I couldn't really squat down because of my age. I'm forty-seven plus I have a swollen ankle. So, I got down like this and coughed." She demonstrated a squatting position. "The guard was screaming get down lower and squat and cough again. She even grabbed the top of my head and pushed me down lower." She continued to explain.

I pretended to be the guard and said, "Cough, cough harder!" We all laughed.

An Indian inmate behind Anya said, "Excuse me, but you just pissed on yourself" as she looked down at Anya's white uniform pants.

I laughed so hard the guard looked over at us to see what in the hell was so funny. Anya bent her head down between her legs and true enough they were wet and pissy. How could she have not felt the fluids coming out of her body? She looked directly at me and said talking loudly as she walked to her to cell to change. "Angie, I am through with you!" I laughed so hard I cried and the other inmates were rolling in laughter too. We all agreed that the cough, cough routine made us all feel like never before, but I turned it into a good hearty laugh for us all versus crying tears from our eyes.

The thought of Anya at 3201 W. Roosevelt in the holding cell bragging about trying to insert some tobacco inside herself to hustle for commissary would have gotten her in some serious trouble. If she had coughed and not realized she had pissed on herself, how did she think her call-girl insides would hold the stuffing of tobacco?

"Cough, squat, cough!" The guard would demand.

"Excuse me guard, who threw that tobacco at me?" She would ask. But yet she blames me for pissing on herself!

While I was writing the guards called for chow-hall. The last supper of the day was around 6:00 pm. It consisted of turkey bologna, corn on the cob, pinto beans, buttered carrots, and a dinner roll. I finally for the first time saw Sherry from 3201 W. Roosevelt walking out of the door.

She smiled and said, "Come to church tomorrow."

The guard said, "You better be glad it was about church."

I nodded my head okay to her. Another inmate pointed her finger at me and asked, "Are you Angie? Damn you are sexy."

I smiled as I got my tray and followed the flow of things. Across from me set a white inmate. She looked at me and said, "You must be Angie?"

"Yes, how do you know me?" I asked.

"Everybody is talking about you being here. They all want you to come in the other barracks. What did you do to have you facing so much time?" She asked. She had short brownish hair, was tattooed up, wore glasses and obviously gay.

I chopped down on a third of the turkey bologna as I opened up the yeast roll and put mustard on it to make a sandwich. I looked at her and waited until I was finished chewing. She waited too wanting me to answer. After I swallowed the thick turkey bologna on the thick yeast roll I looked her in the eyes and asked.

"What is your name?" We spoke softly so the guards wouldn't say anything to us.

"They call me Dicey. Hey, do you know B'Nutt? I was in the county jail with her at 3201 W. Roosevelt." She quickly and quietly asked me.

"Heck yeah, that's my blonde head Bro. I talked to her a week before I got here. We celebrated our birthday together every year. It would have been today as well as Gay Pride, but nothing will be happening because the head leader is locked up. Sad, huh?" I talked pretty fast while sipping on my water.

"Yeah." She said shaking her head.

"Well, they are trying to give me a lot of time and of course I am going to appeal it. So to be honest with you, I am not claiming the time. I haven't signed any paperwork that everybody is asking me about. Do you have a girlfriend in this place? I asked.

"Yes, I'm trying to see her now. She is in a different barrack. That's why I am eating so slowly." She whispered and we both laughed quietly.

"Well, I am really a cool person and that's why people know me. There are so many people asking if I have been here before, but I am not tripping over wanting to be with anyone in here. I am taken." We both smiled.

"Angie, nice meeting you and I am a cool person too!" She smiled and said waiting to see her boo-thang.

"Hey, if you are finished eating go back to your barrack!" The guard shouted.

I picked up my cup and tray and took it over to the proper area. I stood in line to be patted down.

"Turn around, arms straight out, legs apart." The guard demanded as I was patted me down. I assumed it was to make sure no food or contraband was taken from the area. I don't know, but the only thing they could find on me was my disbelief that I was really in prison. I still hadn't talked to anyone on the outside as of yet. I couldn't wait until my baby received some type of mail from me, as well as the other people I had mailed letters to.

What a birthday! Damn it! I couldn't even get a Little Debbie snack cake. I had spent my twelve dollars. Ugh! Plus the list only consisted of things we really needed. We were not privileged enough during the first seven days to have snacks. Not to mention I jumped off the top bunk thinking the guard had called for bedtime snacks, when in fact he yelled, "Diabetic snacks." Ugh!

I walked in a single line, with no talking, staying behind the yellow line and keeping my hands straight down on my sides. I played by the rules as ordered. Some of the officers were no different than those at 3201 W. Roosevelt. You had some that treated you like a human and some that allowed their little authority to get the best of them in their fresh crispy blue uniforms. I know everyone has a job to do and there are rules and regulations no matter what type of situation it is. But do you really have to make people feel worse than the prison time itself? True enough, in many cases it is no one's fault but our own as far as the crimes and making wrong decisions. Or is it the addictions that take over?

I feel that sometimes the system fail a percentage of the inmates as far as giving them the proper help they need. Does anyone deserve imprisonment versus receiving treatment for an addiction or mental issues? To be honest I do not despise anyone, not even the folks that testified against me with their evilness and lies. I do not even despise the court system itself. I have hope on turning this hurricane and unjust sentence around. My life is full of hope and I have plenty to offer the world, especially the LGBT youth. My love still remains solid for my attorney friend, Stanley. It's just a different type of feeling. I know in my heart that if I was in fact his blood relative as much as he claims he loves me, this would have been totally different. All I heard was that it was election time. So, is it true that around election time, some of the politicians want to make examples out of some of us. I can truly see now how the justice has failed several and will continue to fail many others. Where is the goodness in the elected politicians? Steven told me that he didn't work on appeals, but he really didn't see any gaps in my case. I told him nothing other than the gap in my teeth, which wasn't even mine. He claimed he couldn't sleep at night because I am constantly on his mind and that he would get me to Newport quickly. I really appreciate the gesture, but I think every day about the fact that he could have advised me of the consequences of having a jury trial or if he thought my court appointed public defender was properly handling my case and properly advising me. I really felt like love loves no one during times like these. I know for a fact that Steven never looked at my motion of discovery to find any gaps. He sat in the courtroom on the last day briefly. So without having the means to pay an attorney to represent me properly is this fair justice? I whole heartedly love and claim the same love in return. But is it love of business? Would you rather see your "love one" serve twelve years in prison before being eligible for parole?

I wasn't surprised as far as some of the people who I have helped out of the goodness of my heart who haven't written me or put one dime on my books. I'm speaking about some family members, too. I have given, given, given. I have gone out of my way to help others, but I will surely know the next time around. I now realize that I must bless myself and put myself first from here on out. I will continue to pray about it and I finally have the wisdom to say no regardless of my blessings. It's as easy as the elementary ABC's you learn in kindergarten. "I" comes before "U".

AngieSaidThat

I appreciate people like Tweedy, Vona, Kim, Shon, my sister Sharon, Knoxie, and most of all, My Wife. I know that because of the hurricane verdict a lot of people think that because I am in my mid-forties that my life is over. But my GOD has blessed me to realize what my true purpose in life is. Writing! I will make a comeback and my power will be even stronger. My mind will be spiritually stronger and my bank account will be overflowing with blessings. I am writing with a purpose.

AngieSaidThat

If GOD supply the bricks, I promised him I will supply the cement and we will build a mansion together.

It made me proud to watch four of the inmates read the pages that I have written in such a short period of time. Within two days of facing a twenty-one sentence I was on my fourth chapter. I watched an inmate by the name of Heaven read my story that had made the comment earlier, "I checked out three books from the library and I'm the type of person where the story has to get my attention from the very beginning, so I am just going to read my Bible." Heaven was twenty-three years old, 5'2", light-skinned, had pretty hazel eyes, cute deep dimples, short black-brownish hair, thin lips, and a head turner walk.

She and maybe six other women came together from Faulkner County, Arkansas. I teased her about being watched by a stud in the activity area. We both laughed and she said, "Since you are so well known in here, I am going to say I am with Angie just to be safe and I am not going back to the activity room."

I replied, "You can go with me, we will be okay."

In less than one day she had opened up to my personality and sense of humor sharing her charges that were drug related. A lot of women take charges for their men that sometime only get probation.

This was Heaven's first time ever in trouble. She has nine drug charges and was sentenced to only five years in prison, which means she will probably on serve one-third of the time. As she shared her story she also talked about the boot camp program that some of the other inmates tried to talk her into going based on the fact the she may get an early release. They didn't think about the fact that she has anger issues and a smart mouth. Heaven wasn't confident enough in herself that her mental state and loud outbursts

Wouldn't cause her to be shipped back to Newport and her time would start all over again. Thinking that he would be down for her or he had paid all her attorney fees most of these women are ride or die for their men. He didn't do anything for her. Be careful for who you surround yourself with. Sometimes thinking you are in love will cause an imprisonment lock-down around your heart. I claimed Heaven as my niece because I have nieces that are her age. I would give them the same advice. Thoughts flashed back in my mind about how I had asked my court appointed public defender to protect me and my case like she would her new born baby. Her first born baby. Surely doing my two day trial she pumped her titties to feed her baby, but was she preparing to properly represent me? Why didn't she ask that bank teller about a gap. He clearly got a good look at the robber, but she never questioned him as to whether he identified my photo that was shown all over the news. It was my driving license photo. The detectives put a photo line-up together with five other women that had totally different descriptions from me. So surely with the photo all over the news outlets he would have picked me from a photo line-up. I respected the fact that she was pumping her titties to feed her baby, but she didn't even ask the questions I had written down. I know I am not her first born baby girl and she said to me that she was getting paid regardless. Along with her titties, I got milked with ineffective counseling.

However, I explained to Heaven that no matter how others tried to advise her about boot camp, only she knows if her mind can handle the military style prison in Tucker, Arkansas. Only she knows if she is 100% sure her anger issues and following the rules will be a problem for her.

After I asked her to think about being with her daughter again, she cried and cried. I advised her to get it out of her and pray. I advised her to read her Bible and told her we would attend church together in the morning at 7:00 AM. Anyone who knows me knows that I must do evening services, but now time with a purpose waits for no one.

I am thankful that young ladies like Heaven felt comfortable enough to open up their hearts to me. Sometimes it's a persons surroundings that they enjoy that can later lead to imprisonment. So it is truly important to be careful and make wise decisions in life. Heaven continued to read my book. I smiled watching her fully engrossed in my writing. It had her attention from the very beginning. I envisioned my book being in the prison library and everywhere else. Even the Oprah Book Club! I knew the book would make Little Rock headline news. How I wanted to personally get that same newspaper journalist that wrote the big bold printed story about the Little Rock club owner found guilty and sentenced to twenty-one years in prison now enjoying and living her purpose in life.

What happened to all the great community service work I did helping people. Even those I didn't know. Freely giving Christmas presents to children in need, providing school supplies to those in need, raising funds for funerals for those in need and the list goes on and on. Did he run out of room to print all the good deeds I have done for the community even with my gambling addiction?

I will give you the raw truth and the inside edition stories. Inquiring minds want to know. The media has their way of making anyone look bad. It's a job that they get paid for regardless.

AngieSaidThat

Chapter 30

I Want To Go Outside In The Rain

During the evening hours of my birthday I decided within my heart to still bless myself with grace and peace even though I was behind these prison walls. I sat at a table in a real chair for a change instead of the steel iron stool that reminded me of 3201 W. Roosevelt, but the rooms here are much cleaner. Some of the other inmates were watching television or gathered around to talk about their convictions of aggravated robbery, robbery, child molesting, drugs, and many parole violations. Several were repeat offenders, but none had time like mine. Not any of them.

I quietly picked up my chair and moved away from the others. I tried to block their voices out of my head. I pampered myself by simply writing. My spirit remained humble. I can clearly see people on Facebook, Twitter, and Instagram posting comments and speculating about my book. I can see them texting, laughing, and applauding at the comedian in me for writing and sharing stories of my prison life at Newport, Arkansas. Who would ever have thought or believed that I would be facing twenty-one years in prison? I give credit where it is do, and my Creator has promised me a successful appeal and an early release. He has shown me favor and has chosen me out of the millions that are serving prison time. I have let him down so many times and yet he continues to forgive me and bless me with money, the cars of my choice, success and enjoyment as a nightclub owner. I was overtaken by a gambling addiction. Overtaken by what the dice appeared to land on sometimes, snake eyes or deuces. Deuces you are a loser. I lost everything, even my freedom, from a small pair of dice, but the point is not to ever give up. He has revealed to me final test, which is my purpose. He has blessed me with another addiction, writing with purpose.

I have placed this time in my Creator's hand. The State of Arkansas vs Angela Richardson. He never would have thought it? I held down the whole gay community, but this battle overpowered me with no money, an ineffective public defender, and an election season.

But this battle is no longer mine, it is the Lord's! I will allow him to fight for me against the State of Arkansas and all my enemies. We will see the outcome of this hurricane verdict!

AngieSaidThat in Jesus Name!
Amen.

I looked up from writing and realized that Officer Parker had returned from last night. She had the zero tolerance guideline written all over her serious face. I quickly picked up my writing supplies and said goodnight to the ladies. Back to cell# 213.

"No noise!" Officer Parker screamed. She is a black female, 5'7", 175 lbs, had a black ponytail, wore glasses and didn't ever smile at all.

About an hour later she screamed, "Ladies, do not take other inmates items! If you have a black comb, turn it in now! If you don't I will search everybody's cell and if I found out who took it you will be written up!" She screamed looking through her glasses. A strip search over a small black comb? I thought to myself, welcome to prison!

I looked over at my cellmate, Mattie, after our cell was searched and cleared within seconds. She looked at my hair with natural curls and blonde colored hair. I didn't need a comb. I had curls for the girls and blonds have more fun. I use to sag before prison, but now I didn't even want to have fun with any of the girls. A blonde felt numb and was having none of this prison fun.

Mattie is 5'6", 167 lbs, has medium length hair that is above her shoulders due to the fact that in Newport Prison your hair is cut off depending on the length after the cough, cough, squat, long hair don't care nightmare. Her hair damn near touched her butt when she entered these prison walls. We laughed a lot even though we were not allowed to laugh out loud after 10:00 PM. She talked about her slot machine gambling addiction to every casino in town. She lives in Newport and laughed about feeling guilty about gambling so much and took her family to breakfast and lunch at the diner where she gambled.

She is currently doing five years on a drug charge. This is her first time in prison, but years ago on an election day she was sentenced to 365 days in Craighead County. Since then she caught a drug charge and was sentenced to five years in prison, but will only have to serve about six months. She recently got married to a twenty-seven year old black man who is also in jail on drug charges. They got popped in Jacksonville, Arkansas, two weeks after they were married. I thought to myself what a honeymoon waiting on a commissary honey bun!

She openly explained to me that her father was a police officer. He proudly served in his crispy blue uniform. He also got arrested on drug charges, but not surprisingly he beat his case due to tampered evidence. He is still currently working for the city, but not as a police officer. They offered him his position back, but after his experience in handcuffs he never wanted to place another pair of handcuffs on anyone ever again in life. I thought about the old cliché saying, "Be careful what you do to me, cause it may come back on you."

She also shared with me that her best friend was blown up in a meth lab. Again, the evidence was tampered with and because the big time people with money covered it up it was never revealed in the news. She said her best friend was locked inside from the outside and may have been smoking a cigarette that caused the explosion. Wow! Who really believes that someone was actually smoking a cigarette while cooking meth? A hazardous chemically unbalanced drug. The stories I have heard already behind these bars are something else! All I need are the lights, camera, and action. Neither the detectives or legal representatives have the information, but I have all the unfiltered truth and facts.

I continued to read my scriptures, Psalm 58, and powerfully prayed about it all. I looked forward to going to church with Mattie, Heaven, and Sherry. I couldn't help but think about the guard calling for diabetic snack call. I damn near broke my ankle jumping from the top bunk thinking it was a much needed snack, but those calls are for diabetic inmates only. Ugh! I thought to myself, Angie go to bed girl! I knew that if I stayed up writing I would probably miss church. The showers opened at 4:30 AM until 7:00 AM and then reopened again at 4:00 PM until 10:00 PM. I decided to get on up and shower when I heard Officer Parker screaming at 4:00 in the morning, "Chow-chow breakfast ladies!"

To be awake and willing to a shower at 4:30 AM was truly a change for me in a matter of days. Usually that's the time I am leaving the club and on my way to breakfast. I jumped up and prayed with on open heart and mind determined on making it in prison another day.

I got in the shower after signing the log sheet that Officer Parker placed on her desk. We all signed our names and cell number before showering. Showering always give me the awake feeling I needed. With the thoughts I had in my mind I wanted the water to wash most of them away. I applied soap over and over wanting to remove all the dirt that was thrown in my face on June 3rd and 4th. All I could do was sing my good friend, Vona's favorite song by Milira. *"Outside In The Rain"*. I was singing in my head the lyrics;

"I want to go outside in the rain so that no one sees me crying. Oh, I can see so many eyes on me. I imagine what they are saying. They saying I'm a fool, but if they know I am only human."

But I knew the only rain I was going to be getting was in this shower. I finished showering and went back to cell# 213 to go get my writing tablet. It was 4:30 AM and church didn't start until 7:00 AM. I was thinking about another inmate from last night who shared her story with me.

Ross is a white female, 5'4", 155 lbs, had red hair and green eyes, thin lips, and a tear drop tattoo. She had a very funny personality and told me straight up about her drug problem and her crimes of prostitution. I listened and interviewed her as the other inmates watched television on July 20th, the day after my 44th birthday. She is so funny!

Ross started smoking crack at the age of eighteen. I asked her what made her start as she sat down at the table with me.

"I started doing cocaine at the age of twelve." She answered.

"Who introduced you to it?" I asked.

"My boyfriend. He was twenty-one and I was only twelve years old. I did coke every day, period. I started having sex at the age of twelve." She answered.

"Who raised you?" I asked.

"My grandma.   At the age of thirteen I started striping at the 145th Club in Wrightsville, Arkansas." She explained.

"Did you have sex for money in the club?"   I asked.

"No, I would take them out of the club and have sex in the car. They were old black men."   She answered looking at me.

"So, what did this lead to next in your life?" I asked.

"I started smoking crack and street walking on Stanton Road. Did you know there are a lot of drugs and prostitutes on that road?"   She asked me as I continued to writing her story.

I finally looked up at her and said, "No, I didn't, but what was your worst experience?"

"While walking the street I got into a car with a Mexican to have sex.   He wigged out on me, so I gave him back his money and tried to get out of the car.   He jumped out behind me and we fought for about twenty minutes.   I was naked and he bit me all over my face and body. I noticed another car pulling up and so he let me go and I ran.   Some other prostitutes saw what he was doing to me, but not one single person tried to help me.   That was the first time anything like that ever happened to me."   She explained.

I asked her, "What's the worst thing you ever done to someone to smoke crack."

"Me and my boyfriend knocked a Mexican in the head with a sledge hammer and he only had fifteen dollars. We were hot!"   She answered.
"Then what happened?"   I asked.

"We started breaking in houses in rich people neighbor hoods." She answered.

"Do you think you can stop smoking crack and do you miss it now?" I asked.

"Yes, I miss it and if I got some today I would put one in me." She answered.

"Uhm, so what were your complaints as far as the conditions at 3201 W. Roosevelt county jail? I asked.

"The food wasn't worth a damn. There was mold on the walls and the showers were unsanitary." She answered.

"How many times have you been to Newport Prison?" I asked.
"This is my fifth time." She answered.

"Are you serious, five times?" I looked up at her and asked.

"The first time I could have done six months, but I did sixteen months. I got caught up in that gay shit." She explained.

"The second time what happened?" I asked.

"I was sentenced to five years and served nine months, the third time I was sentenced to eight years and served twenty-three months. My fourth time I did a year flat and this is the fifth time for a parole violation, plus I'm facing another gun charge." She explained.

"Do you think you might have AIDS? I asked.

"No." she said shaking her head.

"Why not?" I asked.

"Because I always used protection." She answered looking at me.

"I know that's a lie." I said looking at her smiling. "Stop lying, are you going to keep to real, Ross? This book is the truth. "

We both laughed.

"Angie, fuck you. I am telling you the truth. I promise." She said with laughter. She went on to say, "I might have it. I don't know. I have had unprotected sex and plenty of STD's, but everyone thinks I have

AIDS." If you get caught on the stroll having sex for money and infected with AIDS, you are charged with attempted murder."

"Have you been tested for AIDS in the last year?" I asked.

"Yes." She answered.

"What's the longest time that you have ever been sober?" I asked.

"Six months." She answered.

"So, what do you think caused you to bleed for three weeks at 3201 W. Roosevelt and scared to go see medical?" I asked.

"Drugs and I had a miscarriage." She answered.

"So, how many businesses have you robbed with your boyfriend?" I asked.

"About fourteen." She answered.

"Have you ever shot anybody?" I asked.

"I use to shoot women with BB guns and spray them with mace. I was mean and wanted them to be afraid of me." She said opening up to me with the truth.

"Did you ever use a real gun?" I asked.

"Only on tricks in a rich nail salon on Chenal." She answered.

"How would most react?" I asked.

"They would give me what they had and get the fuck on down." She answered.

"Honestly, how did you feel having sex with different men?" I asked.

"Money talks, Angie!" She said as she slammed her hand down on the table. "I would not stop selling my pussy if I was married to the president." She said.

"I think Michelle Obama got that covered. That's not going to be your way out." I said laughing and then asked.

"Ross, how does smoking crack make you feel?"

"Paranoid. Desperate after three days without smoking crack and that means anything goes. Rob, steal, and even kill to get money." She answered.

"You admitted last night to robbing Splash Car Wash. What was the most money you ever got?" I asked.

"$500.00 to $1,000.00." She answered.
"How did you and your boyfriend pull that off?" I asked.

"We would go steal a truck and ram it into the money box, we would put the money box back of the truck and take it somewhere and use a blow torch to open them. It would only take about twenty minutes." She explained. She looked at me and asked, "Will I go to jail for telling you this?"

"No, I would have to testify against you." I answered.

"I was clean until my boyfriend got out and started back hitting licks." She explained.

"Do you think you will ever stop and change your surrounding of people?" I asked.

"Yes." She said unconvincingly.

"You love your grandmother, right?" I asked her.

"Yes, but we are going to leave her out of it." She said.

"How does she feel about your crack addition?" I asked anyway.

Ross looked up at the ceiling and licked her thin pick lips with a thinking expression on her face. I had touched her heart. Her grandmother was seventy-one years old and the most important person in her life. She finally broke down crying after acting all gangster. *The Cries Behind The Bars*. Ross got up from the table wiping her tears and getting patted down by Officer Parker.   She stopped and wiped the tears from her eyes before walking away from the table, but she continued to cry on her way to church as she stood in the back of the line.   I asked her to pray about her drug addiction and assured her that the devil has his way with all of us.   She walked back over to the table and said.

"Angie, my grandmother provided me with the crack because she said she would rather me be safe and do it at home than out in the streets. She loves me unconditionally.   She watched me smoke crack and we talked like best friends.   She even gave me a trailer with a refrigerator and a stove.   I sold the trailer for $500.00.   I wanted to smoke crack." Tears rolled down her face as she walked off to church.

I had heard about Chaplain Danner from my buddy Yvette, who lives in Dixie, before I even made it to Newport, Arkansas.   She and Pookie had both served time here in Newport Prison.   They both shared their experiences and bragged about how Chaplain Danner was neat, clean, and dressed to impress and his program on the compound.

The moment I walked into the morning church service I saw over two hundred women all wearing white sitting down.   Some were singing and another inmate was displaying the lyrics to the prison church songs on a big screen so everyone could follow along.   After a few songs an inmate by the name of Shirley took me outside of these Newport prison walls.   She gave me chills instantly all over my body.   I nodded my head as I felt the spirit of her powerful voice.   I didn't want her to stop singing.   Shirley is in her mid-sixties, with black and gray hair, 5'4", 165 lbs, dark-skinned with an amazing voice.   After she finished singing I look around and noticed an officer upstairs watching everyone in the white prison uniforms.

I heard an unfamiliar male voice and by appearance only I knew he had to be Chaplain Danner.   He is slim, white, and bald headed, 5'8", 145 lbs, neatly creased purple button down shirt, black slacks, and a black belt.   He spoke clearly and with an anointing.   He never announced his name, but the talk from Dixie spoke for itself. I enjoyed his sermon as he spoke from Roman 23 & 24. He preached about how to treat people with goodness. He preached about how people pray for freedom and soon return back to prison and mostly due to the people they surround themselves with. I can honestly say that I know in my heart I will not be coming back here. I agree with him wholeheartedly that some things are necessary in our lives, but the return of AngieSaidThat will never be at Newport Prison.

Now as far as trying to present certain proposals that I know for a fact will help jail and prison systems on equal rights for LGBT will be a great idea for me to become involved with. True enough, it is not about forcing your homosexual lifestyle on anyone, but no one has the right to tell us who to love. It's time for certain changes and improvements. I noticed there are so many programs to join and get involved in, but what about us? What about our issues? Most programs are pretty much talked against homosexuality. They talk against it not being right. No one has to accept it, but we deserve our equal rights, even in prison. My point of this is with the proper insight, this can prevent a lot of inmates from being written up and losing their classes if they had equality of their rights

Chapter 31

Is It a Crime

Softly rubbing my facing as I was writing I thought about all the homosexuals in prison. What if one of us lost our partner while serving time? Due to the fact that the State of Arkansas will not allow same sex marriages I stood in front of the State Capitol with Judge Gray fighting for LGBT equal rights just one week before my trial.

Now serving time in prison at Newport, Arkansas, I have learned from reading scriptures that Psalm 58 teaches us we are all born sinners. Even those who run in elections have sinned in one way or another. We as homosexuals are loved by GOD, too! Allow Him to judge us on Judgment Day. It shouldn't be a vote on who we fall in love with and want to spend our life with. In the words of the great singer, Sade, *"Is it a Crime."* Sometimes you just can't help who you love!

Why does it take a rich and famous family before someone pays attention? Why is it that even the pastor changes his stance on preaching and teaching about homosexuality when his child comes out of the closet and begin to live their life as openly gay? Not all disown their seed for loving the same gender.

Hopefully, now that I am unable to vote, I can get people involved in campaigning for candidates in the future who support equal rights in the state of Arkansas. It has nothing to do with race. It is simply equal rights for the gay and lesbian community. We matter too!

AngieSaidThat.

Years ago so many people suffered with mental health issues, had serious depression, and committed suicide attempts after being diagnosed with HIV & AIDS. A lot of people would be alive today if they hadn't been bullied and disowned by family and friends. They would also be alive if there were more Awareness programs, but none of the politicians truly care. Even today so many are still having unprotected sex knowing they are HIV positive and are infecting the younger generation. I have seen it happen. I am not speaking or writing about "he say, she say" hearsay. I witnessed it while helping my people in our community and even with a gambling addiction of my own. And let me add I didn't get grant money from the State. I helped an entire community out of my own pocket.

I allowed an associate of mine to use my club to write a grant for funding for HIV & AIDS Awareness. She claimed the funds would be used to hold events to help educate and make changes in the gay community. My job consisted of what I loved to do, planning and promoting exciting events to get the gays to come out and be themselves and enjoy life. Remember how as children being dropped off at pre-school? We all learned from playing and being together. It was my idea of making and creating fun events for the gay community. I was the *only one* that really pulled in the numbers/people trying to raise awareness.

But there are people like Crooksie, who has the ability to write grants full of lies to the Health Department and Community Disease Control to obtain funding under the disguise of raising awareness for HIV & AIDS. She is educated and has an uncanny ability to provide false paperwork and false documentation to get hundreds of thousands in Arkansas state funding. Monies that were used for personal purposes,

184

such as leasing a condo, buying furniture and computers for personal use, paying past due car payments to avoid repossession and taking lavish vacation trips for her and her friends. I honestly had no idea she had been approved for the grant funding until I read an article in the newspaper that mentioned my club in association with her receiving funding for HIV & AIDS awareness. An article full of lies and deceit. She used my business as the site location for all these alleged awareness functions. I nor my club ever received one red cent of the funding she received. She is a snake! She flat out misused the grant funding and the people of the gay community are paying the price for it. They are losing their lives at an astounding rate, yet she still to this day is writing grants and receiving funding to enable her to live in a nice condo and drive a white Mercedes SUV. Money is the root of all evil and she is the epitome of evil! Living the high life off Arkansas state funding and ObamaCare funding, monies that should be used for educating a community and saving lives, and young gay black men are a dying breed. Her heart has never been concerned with what's best for the gay community. It has always been about scamming the State of Arkansas for what's best for Crooksie. Now, again I ask you, *Is It a Crime*? And I answer, yes it is and if anyone should be serving time in prison it's Crooksie for committing aggravated robbery against the State of Arkansas. I also question who is approving these grants. Could it be friends working together to rob the State of Arkansas?

Oh, I know some people are thinking if I am in prison I must have broke the law. Well some break the law big time, but just don't get caught. Crooksie and her inside connections are perfect examples of this! But what the State of Arkansas does not realize about me is that I am worth more and did more for an entire community of people outside of the bars than I am behind the bars. GOD knows it!

Every story in my book is the truth. I'm not the type of person or comedian to make up anything. I turn real life heartbreaking stories into laughter.

Crooksie spoke very well at the conventions on Awareness and ObamaCare. She sold all of us a pipe dream. It truly affects me to know so many of our people are not living to see the age of twenty-five. But who really cares? I just didn't run a club. I had HIV & AIDS Awareness events at the club. I had fundraising events to pay or help pay for funerals and repasts at the club for young men that are deceased because of not having early detection and getting the proper treatment. AIDS is not a gay disease, but a high risk men on men disease. Most are down low and drug users.

As I continue to write after returning from the chow hall my mind took me in several directions. Ross walked over to the table asking me if I was okay and to help her read some of the items listed on commissary. They all walked around in white uniforms excited about being able to shop. I grabbed my writing pad and shopped for words wanting to improve my knowledge to better myself as I challenge for an appeal. I walked to the desk and politely asked for a form to fill out to go to the law library.

Until I'm able to write on my freedom from this unfair sentencing, I am here to do it with hope, prayer, power, and overall continuing my purpose. I picked up a form with the instructions on my way back from the chow hall:

No more than five cases per request.
On the line print clearly below.
Clearly print the specific case requesting;

My first choice...Notice of Appeal 800-42 Circuit Court Pleading.
Second choice...Motion for Reconsideration 800-60.

Third choice...Petition to correct a sentence imposed in an illegal manner.

Fourth choice...Request for transcript 800-18

Every chance I get I go to the Law Library at the Newport Compound to read, learn, and listen. Even with my learning disability I am not giving up.   My spirit of hope and faith will get me a reduced sentencing.

The Psalm of David, the words fill my body slowly and gently and feels good all over and I didn't want to let go.   The words instantly gave me a warm feeling as I opened up my heart.   Well, it may sound like a nice Valentine's Day treat for most, but it melts me like the famous chocolate.

David 25:2-7

I trust in you, my GOD!
Do not let me be disgraced or let my enemies rejoice in my defeat.
No one who trusts in you will ever be disgraced, but disgrace comes to those who try to deceive others.
Show me the path where I should walk, O Lord, point out the right road for me to follow.
Lead me by your truth and teach me, for you are the GOD who saves me.
All day long I put my hope in you.
Remember, O Lord, your unfailing love and compassion which you have shown from long ago past.
Forgive the rebellious sin of my youth.
    Amen

At such a late age I have finally grown up.   My Mama spoiled me and my younger sister,   Meaka.   At the age of thirty-one I felt like a teenager not wanting to begrown.   Sometimes age has nothing to do with decisions if you don't know or understand your purpose in life. Now it all makes sense to me when my friend, Vona, text me asking what was my purpose in life. Wow!

Mama passed at an early age.   She was diagnosed with cervical cancer and died at the young age of fifty-five.   She is truly missed.   She was a woman of wisdom, strength, and faith.   If anybody know me, they knew Mama never failed any of us.   Her health did.   She is truly my hero with wings now.   I much rather be dressed in all white with her inside the pearly white gates of heaven versus sitting in an all white Newport Prison. The thought of suicide facing twenty-one years has crossed my mind a few times, but my Mama didn't raise no fools, and out of ten children, I truly got some of her wisdom and strength. I am not giving up. I have hope and faith!

She made a statement to me that will always stick in my memory and one that I have always tried to fulfill.

"Baby, I want one of y'all to become successful." She said in her last days on her sick bed.

I replied back, "Mama, LaShay and DaShunda have college degrees and skills. In my mind I thought everyone that went to college was successful."

She spoke softly and weakly, "Baby, I know but you know what I mean. Successful." She could barely smile.

She never said it had to be inside or outside of prison walls and me never imagining I would be behind prison walls will not let it stop me from pursuing my successful movements. These white uniforms, gated barracks, messy females, classes being taken or withheld, unnecessary write ups, and even parole violations will not stop me!

AngieSaidThat.

I mean it from the bottom of my heart. I'm not allowing what people on the outside in the streets are talking about or people that will not help me. They claim to love me so much. Yeah, loved all that I have done for them and using me to their advantage. I don't care about the circuit courtroom with the ineffective appointment of counsel. Mama didn't give up after giving birth to ten lovely children without much help from any of the fathers. She strived to make away for all of us with wisdom, strength, and faith. At the age of thirty-five she earned her GED and opened two successful childcare centers. Mama may be gone, but never forgotten.

Chapter 32

Valentine's Day

*F*ebruary 14, 2004. A day we all look forward to spending with your love ones. Having butterflies in your stomach all day while planning something special. Candy, dinner and special presents for your mate.

I received a phone call from my sister, LaShay screaming, "Angie, have you seen DaShunda?" DaShunda is my sister who is eleven months younger than me.

"No, why?" I asked.

"They found her van and her kids haven't heard from her since about 1:00 AM." She screamed.

I continued decorating for my Valentine's Day gala not really thinking too much about it. To be honest, I thought maybe she had a flat tire and her husband, Roadie, picked her up. Nothing more.

On my way to the house, my baby sister, Meaka, called me crying.

"Angie, they found a burned body inside DaShunda's van, but they are unable to identify the body because it is burned so badly. They don't know if it's a man or a woman." She said crying.

It was snowing and cold outside. I slid off the road wanting this phone call to be a bad dream, a nightmare. It felt like I was experiencing a terror movie in real life. Not my sister who was five months pregnant.

And true enough, weeks later it was revealed that it was my sister inside the burned up van. Her husband killed her and their unborn child. He shot her and then sat the van on fire with her inside. His cell phone records placed him at the crime scene in Wrightsville, Arkansas.

Roadie, is 5'8", bald-headed, cute dimples, neatly dressed and a church going man. He was a photographer and quite the charmer, and the ladies really loved him. I found out later and so did my sister as the truth revealed that he also had a man in his life.

Did that cause him to murder her and his unborn child? My loving sister left behind three beautiful and smart daughters. She also left behind a lot of special and fond memories with us all.

Roadie is currently serving life without the possibility of parole. I have thought about writing him several times over the years due to the fact that we had been close at one time and he had taken many of photos at my events.

I want to know why he killed my sister and their unborn child. Surely, three minutes of anger can and will Change anyone's life. It landed him in prison for the remainder of his life.

After all the hurt and pain and not understanding why GOD would allow such awful things to happen to such good people, I felt lost. No one could relate to any of it. True enough, I did excellent deeds for the gay community, but through all the pain and hurt I hid behind a pair if dice.

My focus was on the seven on my first roll or either catching a point and making it before rolling a seven, meaning you are a winner. Shooting dice helped to block out thinking about my Mama, my sister, and my unborn niece and many other hurtful and painful issues. A small square pair of dice helped to block it all out. I had to do it every day and all day until my hands turned red from shooting out of the dice cup. My back ached. Shooting dice eased all my pain. The dice gave me relief that Rolaids couldn't give to gas pains. It was just a type of feeling. I was high on shooting craps! So over the years the more money I made, of course the worst my addiction became.

After my life changing decision on 12-12-12, it landed me in Newport Prison. The prosecutor argued that I thought I had Marty wrapped around my finger and not saying anything. That was not true. Marty actually did not want to give the name of the third person who was with him inside the bank. Due to the fact that I knew he wouldn't do that, I had no clue he would flip it on how everything really took place. The fact is, his lover has a larger gap than mine and a mustache. Why didn't my court appointed attorney Get a dentist to identify the larger gap space in the video shown during my trial? It is not fair that I have been unfairly convicted and unfairly sentenced when I was only the driver just wanting to shoot dice as I did that evening. But after 12-12-12, I never picked up another pair of dice again and I never will. I am no longer in denial about being a part of that 12-12-12 nightmare. I have confessed and admitted to it truthfully to my Creator about the why's and why not's of life.

I feel better, I think better, I want to do better, and most of all I want my entire surrounding to be better. I'm going to pursue my comedy career and continue writing. I will not be the same as I was before. Not because of people, but on the strength of GOD. My Creator has unwrapped my purpose and revealed it to me. It is up to me and only me to show my deliverance and share my blessings in a different way with others.

The club address 3910 will never be the same without me. I know several people tried to get it, and I wish them the best. As much as I dislike KO Dior, Fink, Jo-Jo and Marty's evil lying ways, as a GOD fearing Christian, I love them and wish nothing bad on any of them because GOD has chosen me.

Psalm 58:4

They spit poison like deadly snakes.

I flipped back to Psalm 22:16

My enemies surround me like a pack of dogs; an evil gang closes in on me.

I think about certain people of the gambling house as I read Psalm 22:18.

The divide my clothes among themselves and throw dice for my garments.

The reason I feel like this towards some of the fellows I gambled with is because there were times when I took expensive clothes back to the store for a refund to get money to gamble with. There was a time when I lost four thousand dollars in one day. I didn't always lose though, there were times when I won big! I now know that sometimes when I went to the gambling house after returning my garments back to the store, Jr., Brad, Unbelievable, Greg, and several others had made a "cow", meaning they had pooled all of their monies together to win mine. Dirty! Again, I got milked.

Chapter 33

Prayers over My Book

Another day in Newport Prison serving unbelievable time and waiting on the paperwork to start my appeals. I woke up and quietly prayed. I was trying to cope with the news I received yesterday from Chaplain Danner. I got up when the guard called out activity time about 9:15 AM, I jumped up about 8:00 AM, not sure of the time to do some light exercising to work out the soreness from my body from sleeping on the hard bunk. I washed my face, brushed my teeth, and washed under my armpits and applied Degree deodorant to get myself ready in my all whites. Some of us from Barrack #19 went to the gym. We were in line again with our arms down and walking behind the yellow line. I loosened my body up in room# 213. I worked out on some of the exercising equipment until my body felt a burning

sensation in my arms and legs. This gave me the impression that maybe I was using the equipment properly. I got a blue mat and politely asked a couple of other inmates to join me. We each did about fifty sit-ups. They were both in their mid-twenties, but could barely keep up with my pace. My looks always puzzled people about my age. I pray it continues to do so throughout this storm and over the rainbow.

I noticed the same inmate in the window looking as I went over to get the basketball to shoot a few free throws And talk to Jesus about everything to do with the word "free". It was the same inmate that wanted me to see her in her commissary make-up. As she stood in the window I could see she was all made up today. I thought this was a taste of gay pride after all. She truly had on almost every color of the rainbow, blue, pink and a dash of red. Before I knew it she waived and licked her lips so I could see her gesture. I waived back and noticed her tongue motion. I quickly pulled up on my too big uniform pants in my private area and continued to practice my free throws. I thought about one of my favorite comedians, Kevin Hart, saying he was on the mall and one of his fans said Kevin, we love you and before he knew the guy had blown him a kiss and he caught it. Does that make him gay?

Well, she did the tongue gesture. I was only waiving back because she waived first before she did the tongue gesture. I quickly grabbed the center part of my uniform thinking, "Uhm, did I just get ate out in the Newport Prison activity area? UGH!"

As I played around with the basketball, memories of shooting basketball at Sherman Park Community Center crossed played in my mind. I would much rather be there laughing and talking with my Aunt Renee, who I often think about as well. No one was expecting the Hurricane verdict, but there are some people I am yet to hear from. Yet, I am still thankful and my love remains the same.

As I was returning to the barrack I tried to look outside of the windows in the hallway. I wanted to search For the clouds that Oprah speaks about as I went on back to the barrack to continue writing.

The news that Chaplain Danner gave me when he called me into his office on yesterday was about the home going of Mrs. Washington. I knew it was coming, but sometimes you can't prepare yourself for death of those you truly love.   She had her fight with lung cancer and had finally lost the battle.   My memories of her are untouchable.   Our spirits sometimes give us vibes without being able to be there or being able to pick up the phone and give your condolences.   True, it is hard to cope with the loss of anyone you love while serving time or not.   The memories are priceless and will last forever.   I know that she is in a much better place.   I've lost my two sisters, Kim and DaShunda, plus my hero, my Mama.   I know I now have another angel in heaven watching over me.

Thoughts of the activities in the gym passed rapidly through my mind.   To see so many young LGBT youth serving time was disturbing to me.   What if one of our lovers passed away?   Is it fair that we can't attend their services because of the State of Arkansas ruling against same sex marriages?   So is it a crime to cherish and to hold, to love and to share great experiences, time and memories with someone of the same sex?   Does it have to be an election season to have the right to marry the one you love?   When is all the judgment and racism going to end?   Can't we all just get along?   "Equality", I think as I sit in the all whites.

I may not be able to vote, but I will still get the attention of many and campaign in the future.   I will campaign only for the candidates that are in support for the fairness of it all.   True enough I may suffer from A.D.H.D. (Attention Deficit Hyper Active), but I am still able to get the attention of others.   I am very active and most definite hyper for causes I believe in.   I am not one to suffer from depression or wanting to give up on accomplishing any goals once I set my mind to it.   Yes, it is true that certain struggles and mistakes may have interfered in my destiny, but with faith, hope, and prayer I will conquer destiny even behind the bars.

I forgave my long time "friend" of over twenty years for the lying and misuse of the state funds she collected under the disguise of my club. She will stand in judgment for his misdeeds before GOD almighty.   She is a smart grant writer and able to create the documentation she needed to get the funding she wanted.   Once, I made it my business to report her the head of the Health Department and to others working for the Health Department, but I felt due to the fact that I wasn't college educated or a doctor that my complaints and concerns were overlooked or simply dismissed. Who am I to challenge these professional people? People that I believe were and probably still are working together to steal funding from the State of Arkansas. Nobody and I mean nobody cares! Most of them think we as gays should burn in hell with gasoline underwear on. They think we are ugly and black and have the nerves to love the same sex. How ungodly they say!

Those of the LGBT that are able to love someone, please do it for our sakes and make it count. We matter!

AngieSaidThat!

I sat down at the table that contained forms to fill out on different things we as prisoners need from uniforms, visitations, medical, and etc. I thought about the fact of Ross openly talking about wanting crack behind the bars and her fifth time in prison. Truthfully not understanding or having any expertise of the law, I wasn't going to just accept a verdict of twelve people sentencing me over a damn gap in teeth that wasn't mine.

I looked up and noticed an older white woman with a pink shirt, short pinned up hair, wearing glasses and holding a Bible in her hand talking to some other inmates. I stopped writing and got up from the table and went over to ask her to pray over my book.

She looked at me with an expression on her face that told me no one has ever asked for prayers over a book.

She asked as she stood next to my chair looking down at all of the pages of my books, "What about you?"

I answered, "I need prayer too, but I need prayers over this book to move mountains. Will you place laying hands on my book and pray?"

"Okay, but can you please tell me something about you?" She asked.

"Yes, I sure can. My name is Angela Richardson. I'm from Little Rock. This is my first time in prison and I am trying to appeal for my freedom." I answered.

"Are you a friend of Jesus? Do you believe in Him?" She asked.

"Yes, I sure do and by reading   and studying the scriptures in the Bible for myself in the last few months and really understanding it,   I just discovered that David protected the sheep. "   I answered.

"Well, very good."   She said.

She placed both hands on my writing pad with nearly no blank pages left and prayed as I bowed my head and closed my eyes in prayer too.   She asked Jesus to make a successful movement on my books. She prayed with such an anointing and with power until tears formed in my eyes.   I opened my eyes, but kept my head bowed to stop the tears from rolling down my face.   We both said, "Amen."   I looked up at her and said with heartfelt meaning.

"Thank you so much!"

I asked, "What is your name and where are you from?   I have to put you in my book."

"My name is Marie Vodder, and I am from Heber Springs.   What is your name again?" She asked taking out a piece of paper to write on.

"Angela Richardson, also known as AngieSaidThat"   I answered.

"Okay, I will be checking on you." She very nicely said.

"Well are you going to buy a copy of my book?" I asked.

"Sure, I will." She answered.

"Okay, I will autograph it for you." I smiled and said.

"Okay." She said as she walked off.

Others prayed for their children, some prayed for family members and/or their marriages. I had excitement, joy, and hope all running con-

current inside of me because of the simple fact that she just laid hands on my book and prayed a powerful prayer over it in Jesus name!

Chapter 34

Deliver Me from Evil

GOD placed it on my heart and I couldn't wait another minute. I called numerous times from 3201 W. Roosevelt and left a message the day before I left to come to Newport. I know she gets paid regardless, but I needed to write my court appointed counsel.

Hello Mrs. Copeland,

My name is Angela Richardson. You represented me on June 3rd and 4th in Judge Small's courtroom. I have called you numerous times from the Pulaski County Jail and left messages regarding my appeal. The entire time of the two day trial I was numb. I don't fault anyone but myself for even having to appear in court. However, I do have issues with the court appointed counsel. I wasn't advised properly. First of all, I had no clue or expertise of how a jury trial worked. We briefly talked about a bench trial in which you told me that Judge Bengie Smalls liked you, but he was a hard judge. That statement totally scared me out of a bench trial. I realize now that the judge, the prosecutor, and the public defender are all on the same team working together.

The male teller who supposedly got a good look at the robber, never pointed me out in the courtroom nor did he identify the gap that I have been wrongly convicted over. He obviously saw my driver's license picture that was plastered all over the news to identify me. The detective placed my picture in a photo spread of five women in which not one of us fit the same description. Therefore, surely he would pick the photo that was shown on television the night before.

He clearly made the statement that he thought it was a customer, and so did another teller. I specifically requested that you ask him when he was on the witness stand if he identified me from the news, in which you did not. I also requested you to ask him if he remembered a gap in the suspect's teeth, again in which you did not. The black female employee couldn't identify me as well as being inside the bank. The male teller clearly identified me from the picture in the news and my mouth was closed. Any dentist could tell you that gap was mine, had you bothered to ask. To be perfectly honest, I was the driver. I walk with a very noticeable limp due to an accident in which I was hit by a Little Rock City Sweeper truck that ran a stop sign and am physically unable to run inside and back outside of a bank. Marty provided a third person's name, someone named of Gucci, but not one time did you look into that person to see if he had a gap in his teeth. The person in the bank surveillance photo very clearly had a mustache and it was a man! It was Marty's ex-boyfriend. The prosecutor made the statement that I thought I had Marty wrapped around my finger. No, the third person involved does! The one he protected and flipped the entire story for. That's why it took him over a year and seven months to make a statement and to testify.

Jo-Jo lied the entire time he was on the witness stand. None of his statements matched the statements he made six months after the incident. He and Marty were sleeping with the same man.

I witnessed and so did others in the courtroom one of the jurors asleep in the jury box. I pointed her out to you and you excused it by saying, "Her arm is in the way."

I was acquitted in 2002 in Judge Pecker's court, who is now an attorney. I asked was it not a conflict of interest that he now represented Marty?   He knew the truth about the guy dressed like a female wearing a wig.   He had on a man's pants and shoes, but wore a woman's skirt and scarf.   They all attended Attorney Pecker's church along with Marty's mother, whom I was told I threatened.

Marty's mother called me daily and we prayed.   She admitted to Pecker the truth.

I really got convicted over a gap in teeth that wasn't mine. Someone with larger lips and a bigger nose.

Is this justice served?

Marty has three gun charges, but claims I gave him a toy gun. He is already on probation for robbing rich people's homes.   He gets Robbery – Class B.   I get twenty –one years   for Aggravated Robbery and I never

owned a gun and had no prior convictions and sentenced to serve 70% of a Class Y felony.

Is this Justice or Unjustice?

The prosecutor stated I planned it.   If this was true then why do I not know the third person's name?   I wanted to gamble.   I drove the car and later went to shoot dice.   Two months later I stopped shooting dice and wished for 12-12-12 to just go away.

I should not be serving a twenty-one year sentence.

800-42 Notice of Appeal
800-60 Motion for Reconsideration
800-37 Petition for Reduction of Sentence

The jury was not a jury of my peers. They did not represent my lifestyle and had no understanding of my lifestyle. I did not realize that the jury had no expertise of the law. No one told me, not even You. All you had to offer me was twenty-five years for a guilty plea. I couldn't plead guilty over a gap, but still got convicted for having a gap. It wasn't mine!

Thank you,

Angela Richardson

My mind quickly took me back to the Pulaski County Jail at 3201 W. Roosevelt. I had seen the young blonde Public Defender who assisted Jeannie Copeland on my case. She and another Public Defender were visiting another inmate. I knocked on the window and yelled, "Hey, I need to talk to you about my appeal, and have Jeannie to call me." She nodded her head as if to say okay, but it never happened. Again, she was paid regardless of how she ineffectively performed her job. It's just a job to most with excellent benefits.

I really missed a few people at 3201 W. Roosevelt. I prayed that Hot Pepper and Tippy's sentences were not too unbearable. I can honestly say that my gambling addiction was all about shooting a small pair of dice out of a brown small cup.

I wanted to study the law due to my ignorance of the law during my trial. A lot of defendants have no knowledge of the law and just do not understand the proceedings. But this lack of knowledge should not result in a twenty-one year unfair sentencing that's based mostly on lies and a flipped story. The world against Angela Richardson.

Now I am writing with purpose and I will still mentor the younger LGBT that are troubled as well as the untroubled. But, I am anxious to read, study, and ask Questions to help the next person, not that I will be getting paid. I care from the heart and always have for the entire community.

I had to learn the hard way that you don't always get the love, respect, care, and help from others that you have put into other people's lives. I later realized if I had put all that time into GOD and myself versus pleasing everyone else what a difference my life could have made. I had no real purpose in life then.

GOD is a jealous man, and he chose me, but the Devil had me for so long by feeding me lies that I needed to shoot dice and do evilness if I couldn't get the money to gamble.

I stopped writing yesterday to help Ross read and fill out her commissary list. That's why I allowed myself to move into Room 206 at 3201 W. Roosevelt with Tippy and to sit outside close to Rea-Rea and Leah. The devil attacks our weaken spirits with drugs, alcohol, sex, arson, money, shopping, gambling, and many more addictions. These obsessions and addictions can easily enter into our spirits.

The enemy, Fink, whom I have gone to church with and all those that I have helped to applaud my unfair sentencing. Most people wish evilness upon other people. The wicked has a way of helping the devil. I was a team player with my gambling addiction, but know that I am free from the crap table, I am also truly free of all the evilness. My true purpose in life was revealed to me at 3201 W. Roosevelt. I couldn't get the text I received from Vona out Of my mind and finally I understood it. She text me and simply asked. "Do you know your purpose in life? You need to find it." How will I ever be able to thank my friend?

That text message had me searching, but my purpose readily exposed itself to me in jail. My hope and faith exposed my talented writing skills and my funnier than ever comedic skills. I was known for my comedy shows, but if I could bring a smile or laughter to prisoners in such a dark place, I knew that I was truly blessed with GOD given skills. Prisoners needed to laugh even if they didn't want to and I could make it happen without even really trying to. The system may not believe it or may not even care, but of all the work programs, if you are eligible to participate in them, or the classes that are offered, why not offer a comedy show or a talent show once a month? Do the prisoners not deserve to laugh to ease their mind, body, and soul?

I once got paid for it, now I am providing laughter for free to ease the pain of those that are missing their children and their families and I have never felt more rewarded. Some will never see their families again and some will die in these white uniforms, but I have brought a smile to their faces and put laughter in their hearts. To make someone smile or laugh is priceless to me. Thank you GOD for blessing me to be a blessing to others.

It is not always about the money. My attorney friend, Stanley, who claims to love me as if I was his very own, would have represented me if I had been able to come up With $10,000.00. True enough he has helped me in the past with my club business, but does the love of money overrule unconditional love and giving advice with your expertise of how a jury is selected and what the potential outcome could be? He did tell me at 3201 W. Roosevelt to never give up or lose hope.

I could have gotten $10,000.00 from a buddy of mine, but only if I would have had sex with him. Due to the fact that I have never been sexually active with a man, giving up my virginity for 10,000.00 was not on my list of things to do. I would have needed a muscle relaxer and some form of Xanax to have gotten through it. Overall, I respected my body. I have a body that a lot of women are spending money to have. I have a very nice shape and most women pray for an ass like mine. But, he or his money were not reason enough to" throw it in a circle." UGH! A few other men had asked and offered me money for sex, but all money ain't good money. Some money just ain't worth it!

Damn it! Where was Ross at the time I really needed her? Just kidding!

Chapter 35

Chow Time

　　While I was writing, my name was called to sign for mail.　A young white inmate walked to the door with paperwork in her hand.

Mail 1:　Copy of Motion or Petition to the Prosecuting Attorney
Mail 2:　Copies of Motion of Petition to District or Circuit Clerk along with the Informal Pauper Form

　　Truthfully, I had no idea of the meaning, but the Law Library requested the forms be picked up before any other forms or after chow-time.　I didn't care about the ADC health, beauty shop, request for ID change (on my horrible picture), laundry information, money slips, or commissary forms.　All I wanted was the Law Library forms for typing and copying forms from the Arkansas Department of Corrections.　After I got the forms I treated them the same way I did on my first day of getting to shop for stationary supplies.　The only difference was I knew exactly what to do with the pen and paper, again it's the law.　Due to my learning disability, will the system fail me on studying how to get a reduced sentencing or reconsideration?   Well, my spirit wasn't going to allow me not to try because not all of the Justice System agrees with the unfairness and grant equality.   Some are just not doing it because they are going To "get paid regardless".   Just a few, a very low percentage actually care.   I believe that GOD will place my appeals in the hands and hearts of those that do care about my unjust sentence given to me on June 4, 2014 in Judge Bengie Smalls courtroom. GOD knows I had no clue on how a jury trial worked.

The food in Newport Prison is much better than that at 3201 W. Roosevelt.   I stopped writing as the guard yelled, "Chow-time."   Even with being finally moved from the County Jail in Little Rock, I truly missed a few people, but the dog-chow trays they served were a "P.V." punishment in itself.   I am not speaking parole violation; I am speaking Pulaski County Violation!   AngieSaidThat, Doc!   Time for a change in the kitchen, Boo!

It was wonderful to be able to get a piece of watermelon, pineapples, baked chicken, and good yeast rolls, but the day I saw the menu consisting of of Ala King Chicken with small pieces of chicken in something that looked like a mixture of rice or oatmeal was too much for me.   The guard called it "A Chicken Killed A Convict Special."   I am thankful for the things I am able to eat here, but the chicken killing the convict thing was truly a no-no and the Salisbury steak, OMG!   A truly thick chunk of soft beef.   NO, no baby!   I ate my cookies today and drunk a cup of water, praying for ice someday, and back to writing until commissary arrived.

"Angie, look over at me."   Cough, Cough, Squat, Pissy said to me.   LOL.   "Angie, how are you going to be

Able to survive in here eating like that?" She asked as she grabbed the meat from my tray quicker than a mouse taking cheese from a mice trap. She knew the rules regarding no giving or taking food.   If caught doing so depending on the guard on duty, you were either written up or sent back to your barrack.   I had to get use to all these rules.

Chapter 36

Rules Of Prison Survival

12:30 AM -   Count time…officers does a head count and inmates must be on their bunks.
   1:45 AM -   Kitchen workers report
   4:00 AM -   Wake-up call

   4:30 AM -   Showers open/breakfast begins
   5:30 AM -   Count time…must be on your bunk
   6:30 AM -   Count time/shower closed…(so what if you're musty after activity, it's prison.   Stay out of trouble!)
   6:45 AM -   PIE Program
   7:00 AM -   Beds must be made, area cleaned up, and field squad
        (Lord, please help me to get better with the bed being made properly. I am already facing a life sentence over a gap and this bed will

get me a lethal injection. Not to mention the AM times. Jesus did a lot in the dark. I will pray in his name.)

7:00 AM - Diabetics snack (the call that I jumped off my bunk over not realizing it was for diabetics only, I just wanted a damn snack, it's prison!)

7:30 AM - School turns out…I must get involved

8:30 AM - Barracks Inspection

9:00 AM - Kitchen workers report…2nd shift

9:30 AM - Count time…no way out of these doors but the correct way with all the counting and with so many of us, do you ever forget to carry your mathematical "one"?

10:30 AM - Kitchen workers report

11:00 AM - Chow time begins (it's the chicken ala king for convicts…UGH!

12:30 PM - Vo-Tech & school (I will be involved)

1:00 PM - Field Squad (I'm catching hell)

1:30 PM - Count Time (I'm here reunion)

2:30 PM - Diabetic Snack (okay I now know to stay on my bunk!)

4:00 PM - Dinner (the chicken that killed the convict earlier, the guard shot it and served it to us convicts. I'm hungry!)

4:30 PM - TV's on weekend and holidays until 9:00 PM

5:30 PM - Count Time (so the guards are excellent in math)

6:30 PM - Count time Inmates can unmake beds and get under covers…(do you want to go nite nite, nigga? In Kevin Hart's voice)

7:15 PM - Kitchen clean up

8:00 PM - Diabetic snack…(can a nigga get a bite?)

10:00 PM - Floor crew out

10:30 PM - Kitchen clean up…the convict the chicken killed at 11:00 AM…no evidence, just another death in prison.

10:30 PM - Lights out/showers closed…(you wanna go nite nite nigga?)

Prison awareness to all you game lovers. This is not the place to be if you love electronics. Stay out of trouble and be careful of your surroundings.

You may check out one game per week and you must submit a request to recreation no later than Wednesday.

So, if you love playing your games and your freedom is important. No game station, X-boxes, or cell phones. I have only seen the game "Life" and "Sorry". Facing twenty-one years in prison and these are my choices of games. I thought about *Wheel of Fortune* and needing a vowel. The letter "I". I don't think so game room. Ugh! I need my sentence reduced. I need justice of fairness and equality. I need my freedom rightfully back by law. This is not a game. Should I as an inmate be responsible for the game loss on how the jury trial work and damaged on sentencing verdict? This isn't a place you want to enjoy games. It's not a game!

AngieSaidThat

As I continued writing, Officer Nobling, stopped making her rounds and looked at me with her big brown pretty eyes.

"So, you still writing?" She asked.

"Yes." I smiled and said. Thinking the shifts has changed and she is back on duty but my pen never clocked out.

"I have noticed already that you a mentor in here. I really believe someone is going to get your book published." She said smiling and also asked. "What are you writing about?"

"My life. My experiences. Others. Prison. And listen, I owned a black gay club in Little Rock and I have Performed in comedy shows, but I had a friend to ask me about my purpose in life. I didn't have one. I didn't even know what that meant. I battled a bad gambling addiction. My life finally makes sense. Now that I am here, I speak clearly."

I explained to her my situation. She had to make her rounds, but came back to the table wanting to hear the story. She cut her radio down to tune in. She advised me not give up on my appeals and how the system is failing some people. Her words sent chills all over my body, but I truly thanked her for listening and caring, and not simply because she was getting paid regardless.

"Count time!" She yelled.

I really was impressed on how the other inmates and guards made sure my chair wasn't ever taken. Even one of the guards, after I showered, demanded the chair be returned back to the table so I could write. I was like, Wow!

Never the less, there has been criticism about me coming to prison. The newspaper article lied, the prosecutor information isn't true on the statements that Jo-Jo testified to, or the teller. How is it that a black person couldn't identify me or the Mexican? It took my picture, without the famous gap showing, being broadcast over the news for him to identify me. I can't run. Jo-Jo made a statement about he knew it was me from my walk. He and everybody know I walked with a limp because of a car accident. The detective took pictures of my supportive Black polo boots, but the person seen in the video walked and ran with movement.

UAMS has all my medical records with Dr. Thomas, which states I am not able to stand for long periods of time, run, skate, or wear certain shoes. But who cares? Just another case closed. Not one time did the detective investigate or look for any of the names Marty told him about or Jo-Jo gave to see the third person's gap. They got paid regardless.

So many people have been treated unfairly on sentencing of crimes. We even have innocent people that are in prison, but some get comfortable in the system or jail or in prison relationships and want to stay behind the bars trying to maintain relationships or doing stupid stuff to be in another worse punishment "Seg" area. I've seen it so soon.

I walked over to three white young gay studs, meaning they look like boys. Fems are gay women that are in touch with their feminine side.

"Hey, come here, this isn't a gay club and you have to play by their rules. True enough we are going to be watched, judged over our lifestyles, but there are rules to be followed. We already don't have LGBT equal rights in here. Y'all need to chill. So, your girlfriend is in "Seg" and you got caught flashing her. Stupid!"

"Well, yes." She answered, but carefully listening.

"Look, play by the rules. You don't want to be locked down no more than we already have to be. We walking around looking like a lot of mixed up queers. Follow the rules. Catch her in the activity room and talk without a write-up and being locked down." I said smiling.

"It's not easy for us in this state being openly gay as far as our rights are concerned. You guys are in prison and we have a lot of rules to follow, so let's do so okay, guys?"

All three stood in front of me with their short hair cuts, in their early twenties, tattooed up and thanked me.   I assured them I have a listening ear and was opened for any questions. I walked back to my writing area and continued to write. My thumb formed a dent in my upper skin from writing so long.

To actually listen to these people coming in and out of prison repeatedly weakened my stomach. Some stated they will be back. To see Ross' paperwork for the fifth time back was crazy. I'm facing a lifetime due to not knowing and being wrongly advised and several people have aggravated robbery charges and will probably serve 2 1/2 years of a fifteen year sentence. Some in "robbery boot camp" and will be out in eight months. So, yes this book needs to be prayed over in Jesus name for justice!

I looked out through a very small window on the door in Unit 19 which was facing the "Seg" room that separated us with locked door and a guard watching monitors and the inmates. I saw the wires of the fences that Surrounded the premises shaking. The heavy rain and wind made sounds of a thunderstorm. The television flashed severe weather warnings. We lined up for chow hall. I overheard inmates whispering that nothing can knock this building down, not all of this cement. I turned around in the chow line before entering outside to the yellow line with my arms down thinking, so, you would think GOD can't move cement, huh? He moves mountains. I smiled thinking about my mountains.

We walked into the chow-hall and the smell of the fishy odor assaulted the hairs in my nose. As gay as I am, I never in life smelled anything like it other than the odors at 3201 W. Roosevelt during the last days before arriving at the prison. We were being served a fish patty that reminded me of an old nasty sausage with a fishy order, pinto beans, and the famous yeast roll. I ate my roll and enjoyed the taste of the ice finally in the water. True enough, sodas are listed on commissary, but they are not cold or we can't have ice. What a refreshing taste of a hot Dr. Pepper! What happened to the old fashioned saying, "I drink Dr. Pepper and I'm proud!" Ugh! The prison system even took away the commercial's refreshing taste of a cold Dr. Pepper.

Chapter 37

Equal Justice for All

One more day before I receive the items   I ordered from commissary.   After leaving   the chow-hall earlier, I knew that I had to keep some type of money on my book.   I felt the first couple of months, even the first couple of years that I would be okay on money. But who will really continue to think about you facing twenty-one years and not eligible for parole for twelve years?   It's been a week as of today that I haven't heard from my Baby, but I am thankful to those that have mailed me letters.   Last night I received mail from my ride or die, Tweedy, and my play niece, Candace.   I knew that others would write within time, but what was My Wife doing that was so important other than me hearing from her?   I better get a letter tonight.   My mind was puzzled.   I know she allowed her work to stress her out on top of the fact that her hot stud is in prison with over

eleven hundred women.   Already, I've been told not to drop the soap. Well, I did drop my bar of Dial soap and I left it and went back to my bunk.   My name is already ringing and folks asking, "Where is Angie, the blonde head with the curls?"   I knew my nice big booty, flat stomach, perfect round titties, and nice brown skin had them wanting to see what I try mostly to cover up.   But, I knew my milkshake would bring the girls to the yard, damn right it's better than yours. The love of my "gap!"

Easily over blessed with such a great sense of humor and personality, I tuned into listening to the mail call. I received a returned mail notice regarding a letter from Shon. It contained six photos, but only five allowed and a letter too large to fit inside a regular size envelope. There was a note requesting I send a signed inmate check for the amount of seventy cents to return to sender.

I walked over to another inmate trying to clear my mind of the mail calls, money receipts, phone account and the world on the outside of these bars, period. I am facing entirely too much time to worry about all those who claimed to love me so much. I will continue to write with a purpose. As long as I am able to request the Law Library forms, my prayers, faith, and hope is all I need to get a fair sentencing reduction.

I walked back over to the table and asked Mrs. Woods to share her stories that led her to imprisonment. She is a black female, fifty-four years old, short black hair, 5'3", 178 lbs, and missing a tooth at the bottom and a gold tooth in her mouth.

"Mrs. Woods, is this your first time here?" I asked.

"No, I've been to prison twice before. I'm back on a parole violation." She answered.

"What happened?" I asked.

"First time was for theft of property, I was sentenced to three years and served six months in Tucker, Arkansas. But I was already on probation for twenty years for killing a man." She explained. "The second time I was charged with Second Degree Murder. I was sentenced to twenty years and served five and a half here in Newport." She explained.

"Where are you from?" I asked.

"Texarkana." She answered.

"How many children do you have?" I asked.

"Eight." She answered.

"So, tell me about the murder charge, please?" I asked.

"Well, I was at my home and I told everyone to leave, but this one guy came back. He was a friend of the family. He was trying to get some drugs from somebody and I asked him to leave." She explained.

"Did you all start arguing?" I asked.

"Hum, yeah, I asked him to leave and he wouldn't leave. He acted as if he was about to pull something out on me, like he had a gun or some kind of weapon." She sat up in the chair explaining. "So I went into the kitchen as we argued and got a knife and stabbed him in his back, everywhere I could." She explained.

"What happened after you repeatedly stabbed him?" I asked.

"He ran out the door and down the street. He fell down and died. The police came and the ambulance picked him up." She explained.

"How did they know you did it, Mrs. Woods?" I asked.

"The blood led back to my house." She replied.

"Did they arrest you the same day?" I asked.

She nodded her head and answered, "Yeah."

"What happened after that?" I asked.

"I went to jail and sat for nine months before I bailed out on a $10,000.00 bond. I got twenty years probation. I violated the probation and they sent me to prison." She explained.

I stopped writing to make sure I heard her correctly. "So, they gave you twenty years probation on a murder charge?" I asked slowly.

"Yes." She answered.

"Wow! Unbelievable!" I replied.

"They knew I was going to mess up, that's why they gave it to me." She said.

I wrote her story and shook my head at the System itself.

"Mrs. Woods, so why are you here now?" I asked.

"Parole violation, I caught a new charge." She answered.

"What's your new charge?" I asked.

"Robbery, I was offered five years and have to serve six months on a concurrent sentencing." She answered.

"Okay, Mrs. Woods, thank you for openly sharing your story." I said and smiled. I shook her hand and assured her to get a copy of my book coming soon.

I have spent so many years on LGBT events, but I wanted to change for myself on certain logics and decisions on how to become a great writer and a great mentor to my community. My people, black or white, will commend my ideas and my faith and hope, even while in prison, of not giving up on my freedom.

I looked around at all of the women in white uniforms. While conducting interviews of other inmates, I always make sure each one of them feel comfortable Speaking with me. I was getting through to people in ways that people with educational degrees and doctrines could do. GOD used me and I enjoyed the feeling of HIS spirit. Did it take for me to come to prison to fulfill and walk this path for a powerful blessing over a "novel" that is written from the heart of it all.

The reviews of some of the inmates and even telling the officers about my writing skills are exciting to my soul. I enjoyed others saying how they wanted to read it. Heaven even stretched out her arms craving for another page of the chapter. I know without a doubt there are millions of people serving jail and prison time and I can't even think from feeling the spirit of a new found purpose after being sentenced to twenty-one years in prison. I'm ready to share a tasty and delicious slice of my cake with many. I have finally taken steps to bake a cake, but my point is I am doing it. I got enough talent to openly serve with icing on top of the stories of my writing purpose.

It fascinates me the power of AngieSaidThat in the midst of it all. I know in my heart my appeal will be considered for reconsideration on my sentencing reduction. I know my Club Goodtimes @ 3910 would never be the same again. I had great ideas, but I was told by my dad, Nick, that a fool and his money soon parts. But I was also told by my mother, "You are going to be okay. I don't worry about you. You are the strongest out of ten children." Again favor.

I really changed my ways before my trial. So many wanted to know why I just didn't take a plea or come clean. After I stopped gambling with the high roller dice guys, I changed my surroundings and was actually asked to speak at the Little Rock Job Corp on judgment and the LGBT program. To be honest, I called my buddy and a very dear friend, Denise, to ride with me. Also surprising, Kyna, an associate, showed her support with her two lovely young daughters.

I was introduced and walked in to a great round of applause for AngieSaidThat. I freely explained to them that I was there to help with their feelings on being judged, feeling depressed, sex awareness, and overall learning to love yourself. I assured them that once a person gets to know themselves, other things will fall into place. I wasn't there for any of the students to inbox me or think it is okay to come on to me because of my open mind. I just wanted to make the discussion easier and for everyone to be themselves.

The first question was from a young lady.

"So, are you single?"

I'm thinking to myself, "Are you listening or just looking at me?" Ugh! But I smiled answering.

"I'm committed."

Well, that word does not sound too good to me right now, being "committed" to prison, so correction, "I'm taken." However, I enjoyed it so much and I wanted to help our young black and white generation.

The State of Arkansas really needs to understand that even if most politicians don't agree or dislike homosexuals, people deserve to love life. We deserve our rights just as you guys deserve your rights on what you want in life. Stop all the judgment as if anyone is living a perfect life. We all are human! As you congressmen gather around the table, are you voting fairly on bills that should be passed regarding equality.

Is it fair that certain judges have addictions, but I'm serving twenty-one years in an all white uniform over mine? They may not have been driving the getaway car, but is any of it right?

C-800-37 Angela Richardson vs State Of Arkansas

This is an application for relief filed by your petitioner, the above named, an indigent prisoner and the aggrieved party to have reduced your petitioner's sentence imposed by this court. I continued to flip through page #6.

That your petitioner believes himself/herself entitled to a reduction for the following reasons; ineffective counseling, conflict of interest, convicted over a gap that wasn't even mine, unfairness of justice and equal rights.

I just wanted 12-12-12 to go away forever.

I jumped onto the top bunk and read the Bible seeking and praying for guidance on all my appeals and the entire situation before going to sleep confident of my purpose.

Psalm 70:1-5

Please GOD, rescue me! Come quickly, Lord, and help me. May those who try to destroy me be humiliated and put to shame. May those who take delight in my trouble be turned back to disgrace. Let them be horrified by their shame for they said, Aha, we've got him now! But may all who search for you be filled with joy and gladness. May those who love your salvation repeatedly shout, "GOD is great!

But I am poor and needy. Please hurry to my aid, O GOD. You are my helper and my savior. O Lord, do not delay.

"In Jesus name, goodnight." I prayed.

I placed my first paperwork on Appeals in the Bible on Psalms 58. This battle is not mine. Justice. The system has failed many, but GOD, helped plenty!

AngieSaidThat

Chapter 38

Hustle & Flow

Morning, noon, and night, I plead aloud my distress and the Lord hears my voice. He rescues me and keeps me safe from the battle waged against me, even though many still oppose me. For my enemies refuse to change their ways, they do not fear GOD.

As for these friends of mine, (Marty, Fink, & Jo-Jo), they betrayed me; GOD's words are smooth as cream, but in his heart is war. (I'm still successful), His words are as soothing as lotion, but underneath are daggers.

I woke up and read some scriptures. Psalms 55:17-18 & 20-21, made me feel as if I had been called for my very first visitation from my Creator to prepare me for the days and months that lie ahead of me.

After doing thirty sit-ups and stretching my body which ached from a very uncomfortable bed, I walked from Barrack 19 Intake area. I thought about the worn and outdated mats, the odor of the smelly sheets and blankets @ 3201 W. Roosevelt and gave thanks to GOD for a better upgrade of living. None of it is what I am use to, but a garbage dumpster is almost better than the County Jail @ 3201 W. Roosevelt.

I talked to my cellmate, Michelle, explaining to her no matter what the parole rules consist of and I can't speak For others, but I will follow the rules and never will I return to anybody's prison. To think about Mrs. Woods last night admitting to me that she stabbed a family friend repeatedly to death and was granted twenty years of probation and I'm sentenced to twenty-one years on a trumped up aggravated robbery charge? I thought of all the stories I have written about from my dusty blue uniform and transferred to Newport Prison in all white as the stories continue with AngieSaidThat sitting at the same desk, but in a more comfortable chair with a cushion, wheels, and with a much better feeling to my back. Jones sat down and wanted to freely share her story. She told me that it will make her cry, but she wanted to share it with me and of course I whole heartedly listened.

I placed both my hands together as my voice trembled. I prayed for the two of us as we closed our eyes on The Cries Behind The Bars at Newport Prison with AngieSaidThat

Twenty-two years old, white female, shoulder length blond hair, 5'9", 216 lbs, cute smile, wore glasses and cheerful. Jones placed a chair on the side of me trying to hold back the tears.

"Let's see how we are going to start this off. What's hurting you so badly?" I asked. "Be honest, even if we shed a tear. It's okay." I told her.

"Not feeling loved. That's what has caused my charges, putting up with a pimp, and my drug addiction. All
Of it." She stated.

"At what age did you start using drugs?" I asked.

"I was about thirteen when I started smoking a little weed and taking pills to fit in with the older people, you know?" She explained.

"Uhm, so how did that make you feel?" I asked.

"This makes me feel like I am talking to a therapist." She said and we both laughed.

"Well, you are talking to another prisoner inmate." I replied.

"The drugs made me feel like I was special and cared about." She continued talking.

"When did you have your first sexual encounter?" I asked.

"At fifteen years old. My friend's husband got me drunk down on the river. We smoked some weed and he raped me." She answered.

"Did you report him?" I asked.

"No, but I told my Dad." She answered.

"What did your Dad say or do?" I asked.

"He wanted to press charges, but everybody in school knew about it and I didn't want to go through all that, the bullying." She replied.

"So, where did this lead you to in your mind and how did you feel in school with others knowing what happened?" I asked.

"After that I started having sex with everybody. I felt like I was wanted and loved. I still do." She answered.

"What drug did you enjoy the most?"   I asked.

"Meth."   She answered.

"Why?"   I asked.

"It made me a different person.   The people I hung out with wasn't shit.   The drugs made me feel like I was a little bit better than them.   I felt good about myself."   She explained.

"So, did you get to the point of having unprotected sex for meth?"   I asked.

"Yes."   She answered.

"At what age?"   I asked.
"Eighteen years old."   She answered.

"Have you ever been tested for AIDS?"   I asked.

"Yes, I have been tested for everything.   It wasn't the sex; it was the shooting up that has messed me up."   She explained.

"Messed you up how?"   I inquired.

"I'm twenty-two years old with Hepatitis."   She said.

"How do you spell that?"   I asked.

"H.E.P.A.T.I.T.I.S."   She spelled out for me.

"What made you turn to a pimp?"   I asked.

"Because the last time I got out of prison I was doing good as far as living in a Christian halfway house, sober, going to church, and working.   And it still wasn't enough.   People who claimed they loved me still expected more from me. So, I started looking for a place to move away from the halfway house. And then I met Rich." She cried and cried as she explained.

"How did you meet Rich?" I asked.

"He had an ad posted online about renting an apartment." She answered.

"Like a roommate type of thing?" I asked.

"No, he was slick about it. It was an ad for free rent for a girl that's money motivated. I knew what he was talking about." She answered.

"How does Rich look? Is he your type of guy?" I asked.

"He is black, buffed, my height, and just sexy." She smiled and said wiping her tears.

"We started talking and he told me that he would help me make something out of my life. I moved in and he became my pimp." She said.

"So, Jones, when was your first job assignment?" I asked.

"The first week I moved out of the halfway house. He went to Dallas and I worked the entire time he was gone." She answered.

"How much did you make in a week?" I asked.

"The first week I did a few free sexual acts and only made about $500.00." She answered.

I looked at her and said, "The Hello Kitty was on clearance, wasn't it?" and we both laughed. "What is the most you have ever made?" I asked.

"Well, I went to Searcy and made $660.00 in one day from one trick." She answered.

"What did you do for $660.00?" I asked.

"Let me check my books." She said and we both laughed. "He got head, we had sex, we smoked his weed and had drinks. I stayed for a couple of hours." She further explained.

"An all expense paid round trip, huh?" I said smiling.

"How much did Rich get?" I asked.

"All of it." She answered.

"Look, how is it that you take chances of catching diseases sleeping with strangers and then you give a pimp all of your money? It's not right, Jones?" I said shaking my head.

"He needed me." She replied.

"Look a pimp can't love his hoes. He's going to do that to other women." I said.

"No, he told me that a pimp would be lying if they said they have never fallen in love with a "hoe." She said crying uncontrollably.

"Jones, so why do you think this man loves you?" I asked.

"He paid all the bills." She said.

"Well, he should." I replied. "You got caught in North Little Rock at La Quinta Inn with several other of his prostitutes." I stated.

"It's different. I have met his family. I sleep in his bed. When I found out I had Hepatitis he would not let me work. He took care of me." She said.

"A "coochie" leave of absence, huh?" I said jokingly and continued. "I heard that pimps don't let their main hoes work and get money for sex. How does that make you feel?"

"Well, we have a game plan. I'm going to work for five years, have his baby and allow his other hoes to continue working." She explained.

"Do you think Cinderella really turned back raggedy at twelve o'clock or they took a commercial break? Do you think it's a fairytale? I asked her.

"I know it's not a fairytale and I know it is going to end badly." She replied.

"So, you are deeply in love? So in love that this heart of yours has a gate locked around it in prison. I'm sure he's thinking pimp style, for the love of money." I replied.

"We have like a hustle and flow type of relationship and love." She smiled. "He loves me. It's just fucked up!"

"How do you meet your tricks?" I asked.

"Online." She answered.

"Were you a part of the North Little Rock Prostitute Bust?" I asked.

"Yes, that's how I got arrested." She answered.

"So, how do you feel now sitting here and not being able to sell your body for Rich?" I asked.

"It's the six months time that I am doing in here. It's the fear of him leaving me. I wouldn't know what to do without him in my life. He writes me and sends me money." She replied.

"How much money does the big pimp send you?" I asked.

"Twenty-five or thirty dollars a week sometimes." She answered proudly. "If I add it all up, it wouldn't ever add up to one bill I have paid for him. He says he loves me because I sell pussy for him."

"Look, Jones, you are in here for being in love with a pimp! As we speak you don't even have $100.00 on your books. This pimp tried sending you paper to write on since you love to write versus putting money on your books. He does not love you! This is really sad." I explained.

"I was molested and stabbed nine times by my first husband. I have been raped. I don't feel good at all about myself. Rich makes me feel special. He won't perform oral sex on me because I sell my body." She said crying uncontrollably again. "But, I love him so much and I can't help it!"

"So what if he leaves you while you are serving time?" I asked her.

"I am going to hurt." She replied. "I'm good to him. I even give him the change. I couldn't even have the quarters, dimes, nickels, or pennies. Rich got all of it." She explained.

Ross butted into the conversation and said. "You are stupid! I stopped selling my body so my man could give me some head and we smoked plenty of crack. We are going to get y'all to the room and rob you and Rick." Ross teased.

"Rick don't allow me to sell my body to black men." She said.

"Why can't you date black men?" I asked.

"Most black men don't have much to lose. I only do tricks for rich white men. I got twenty-one felonies, but certain judges like tricks too." She explained.

The more I tried to convince Jones that Rich would never marry her and she would be replaced by another call girl, the more in her mind she felt as if she was a special "hoe" to Rich. She justified all his actions and how he sent her just enough money in the County Jail @ 3201 W. Roosevelt to get cigarettes, shampoo & conditioner. Nothing more and nothing less as long as he was taken care of her, even if another "hoe" had to do it. She felt love. He told her all the right words she needed to hear. She's a special "hoe" to her pimp. So special she would repeatedly come back to prison for something she wasn't doing for herself, but for the love of Rich, who claimed he was making a life for her. A career as a low budget call-girl. She feels loved and wanted by her Pimp Rich.

Before, we stopped talking, I asked her to get back into her Bible and try loving herself. I reminded her that she's smart and beautiful and it shouldn't take a pimp or anyone else to insert that inside of her head and to feel it all over her soul. The fact of having to lay down with strangers and the fat men she cried about as she placed herself on top of them. Even being high couldn't ease the feeling of sadness of making money for Rich and even giving him the loose change from the bottom of her purse. So thinking of Hustle & Flow, is it really hard for a pimp? I thought about how six months after her release, she will be back

228

making Money for Pimping Rich.   Her drug addictions are stopped for now to make Rich happy versus herself.

I looked up and gave praises to Jesus.   I am thankful for being given the opportunity, like a candidate from this past voting season, to get others to listen, to share real stories, to share their cries, and their trials and tribulations.   Pure excitement runs all through my body to actually write about them.   It also made the inmates feel special, important, and cared about just to be considered for being in the book.

I understand that I have been sentenced to twenty-one years in prison unfairly and even the Crispy Blues agreed on that.   Who do you know that has written a book in less than two months behind the bars versus being depressed?   Nobody!   I licked my lips and talked to the Higher Power, thanking my Creator.

My Creator instilled this in me.   It is a gift that I have always known that I possessed, but I blocked it out do to my gambling addiction and my relationship with the devil himself.   I am thankful to my dear friend who text me about finding my purpose and encouraging me to read the scriptures.   I'm living through faith and hope and I understand the power of prayer.

Chapter 39

Three is a Crowd

It's only My Creator. It's Him. Jesus. I was talking to GOD about my situation. It is all going to work out in the name of Jesus. I know that faith without works is dead. I must make steps first in order for Him to make steps in my favor. So many in the Bible experienced prison, but GOD worked it out for them and he can do it for me too! I will not do the time that twelve unknown jurors, who were not a jury of my peers, imposed upon me. A sentence imposed upon me over a gap that wasn't even mine. Those twelve people had no clue about my lifestyle as a homosexual. I promise you this book is going to be the most talked about book in history. What makes me smile is that people will laugh even though it really is a sad situation at heart. Cough, cough harder, squat!

GOD allowed me to have fingers. Some inmates are serving time without fingers, legs, eyes, ears, or totally 100% disabled. I'm blessed without being able to spell correctly, but able to write about others as well as AngieSaidThat.

It's not based on just my lifestyle or my opinions of others or the system. This is based on Equality and the GOD's honest truth and fairness for all American people. My spirit and GOD has assured me that my appeal will be Granted, but the devil has a room inside these prison walls too. If I have to do twelve years of a twenty-one year sentence, it will not be without a fight to mentor the young LGBT troubled youth, it's not without continuing to be in my nieces, Bailey and Madison's lives, or without fighting to speak out to our community about HIV & AIDS Awareness, prison awareness, and staying out of trouble.

It is not because I failed. It is only because I'm just another black person that couldn't afford an attorney and wouldn't sell my body to get one. Even with a gambling addiction most men wanted to sleep with me on some days that I lost. Big time money offers to sleep with me. Hell no! I can't take back some things I have done in my life, but I cherish my body. I have learned the fear of healing is a failure. The fear of overcoming any addiction is a failure. I am doing whatever it takes, but will the system fail me on justice.

800-44 Motion of Reconsideration
800-37 Petition for Reduction of Sentence and Motion for Appointment of Ineffective Counsel

The Public Defender's statement that she "will "get paid regardless" if I am convicted or not at trial replays repeatedly in my mind.

Even sitting in Newport Prison, I watched as one door closes and the next one opens to a different area. Surely if one door closes on my situation, I will fight to open another one. My case was closed with the facts of a third party. Marty gave the name to the judge and the whole courtroom. I can't say that it is his ex-lovers true name. The bank surveillance video shows two people entering into Metropolitan Bank. Marty's face is clearly revealed on camera. The second person has a gap, large teeth, and a mustache. The suspects ran out of the bank.

Medical records will prove I can't run. I walk with a limp, but I am framed by the gay men.

"Three way love affair." The lyrics of a song by Milira. *"I don't want to be caught up in a three way love affair. Don't you know that there is a crowd?"*

Nevertheless, I never thought the story would be flipped a few weeks before the trial and almost two years later, but even Marty's attorney, who was once a Little Rock judge and acquitted me in 2002, was known for helping young gay men in bad situations. So if he did it, as a judge sworn under oath and now practicing as a smart attorney with expertise, it is easy to see that I was really railroaded. His client, Marty, was already on probation with three gun charges and was seen on the video with a gun in the bank, but his charges are dropped to robbery on a plea deal. Then he lies about who went into the bank with him. The amount of money they supposedly got speaks for itself.

The big bold printed newspaper article speaks about it and I was the bank gap tooth bandit, so I would've known All the plays on the large sum of money, wouldn't you think? The entire stories Marty told in court didn't make sense, not to mention that Jo-Jo couldn't keep up with all of his lies that he was advised on by the confidential informant, Fink Tillery, who was sitting in the courtroom dressed in his off duty police attire. The Little Rock Police Department impersonator.

Two detectives knew he played the dream night role of a police impersonator, but who took action? None of them! He's a snitch for them to make their jobs easier. Another case closed.

I was no longer sure about anything in life. I couldn't even talk to the detectives that stood in my face spitting tobacco that was stuffed in the bottom of his lip. First question he asked was, "Are you a fucking racist?"

He openly speaks in the Motion of Discovery about how this confidential informant helped with another case. Fink gave them all the information on Marty to get the heat off of his ass for impersonating a police officer.   Fearful that I would tell it on him and about his molestation of teenage boys he pulled over by flashing a blue light and a fake police badge.   Some of the teenagers were afraid of being pulled over by black police officers and out of fear would agree to Fink suck their dicks so he would let them go.   True enough, I reported his actions, but do to the fact that he is now a paid confidential informant, a snitch, nothing has been done to him and he is probably to this day Impersonating a police officer and molesting young boys.   Justice for all!

Jo-Jo was the mastermind behind installing the blue police light in their Impala or Chevy Caprice. During the early week of a cold December month, Marty was arrested while test driving a Chevy Caprice with Jo-Jo behind him test driving another car as well.   The three of them enjoyed picking up young boys.   They even fell out with each other for sleeping with some of the same guys.   Most gay men call it "Trade", which means the men/boys they are sleeping around with are down low.   They are either married or have a girlfriend.

To make a long story short most of the gay community say Jo-Jo is the one that turned Marty in to the U.S. Marshalls for cash two weeks after the 12-12-12 incident when he returned from Dallas spending time with the very person he lied to protect, on June 3rd & 4th, 2014.   True enough, I accepted his calls, but I also asked him doing a recorded call at 3201 W. Roosevelt if they asked him if I was the one inside the bank with him.   He stated, "I couldn't look you in your face and lie on you like that."   The public defender assured me the phone call would be played in court, but of course that was a lie.   None of the recorded calls were played for the jury to hear.   The only thing the jury got to hear was the prosecutor drilling me about talking to him on the phone, but never mentioned the course of the conversation.   But again, they all get paid regardless.

Chapter 40

Who Threw That Ham At Me?

The guard walked by looking as if I had said something after my name was called several times for mail. The other inmates call it "fan mail for AngieSaidThat."

I looked at Officer Story and said. "I'm T.I. around here, Sir. "

"Well, you need to write a book about this place." He replied.

Officer Story is in his late forties, 5'8", 190 lbs or more, grayish hair, wears glasses, has a gut on him and had a very humbled look on his face as I replied.

"Sir, I am writing a book. Hold on, let me show you something." I smiled at him showing my gap of conviction.

I walked over to the desk and picked up over 132 pages that I had written in just one week in prison. I walked back over to his desk and showed them to him.

"Look, this is it. Are you going to buy a copy?" I asked.

"I want you to give me an autographed copy." He answered.

I smiled and said. "Okay, Sir, I will do that just for you."

I walked back to the desk that I claim as my interview area. The other inmates respected my writing and interviewing area as well.

The earlier excitement of the day kind of distracted me from writing, but I decided to not feel guilty about it. I was only taking a break for a few hours from my purpose of writing.

Today was our first day in a week to go outside for one hour of activity time instead of going to the gym. I laid my supplies down on the desk in cell# 213. The brightness of the sun hit my eye; the freshness of the humid air graced my spirit. I looked up and noticed the men prisoners on top of the building working on the roof as a guard watched them.

I started walking around the tall wired gated fence. Walking and praying at the same time. No sights of nothing but fields that I would soon be introduced to wearing a white hat with fabric attached to the back and hard worn out boots on the field squad, also known as the hoe squad. I didn't know how I was going to be able to do it with my bad right ankle and not being able to stand for long periods of time. I will just have to pray about it until that day comes.

Some of the prisoners played volleyball, basketball, or just chatted with one another. I walked around the Fenced in yard three times and then I went over to Mrs. Spencer, the officer over the activity area and asked her if she remembered my buddy, "Y".

Mrs. Spencer has long black hair, wears glasses, in her late forties, 5'5", 165 lbs, and a sweet lady.

She smiled and replied. "I sure do. How is she doing?"

"She is doing great. She is raising her oldest grand baby and she is a good friend of mine." I answered thinking how bad I wished I was in my buddy's back yard in Dixie drinking a cold Bud Light and running across the yard to visit Ma, who has spoiled me with her cooking and snacks. Through it all, I know they truly love me.

Sometimes it is the best feeling in the world to make others laugh. I walked over to the table with five other women in white uniforms talking. One was on a parole violation for shoplifting. I joined in on the conversation and shared a story about my cousin shoplifting.

"Hey y'all my cousin went into a Kroger store around Thanksgiving one year wearing a long dress. She placed a ham between her legs and tried to leave the store. As she was walking out the door the ham dropped out right in front of the security officer. She turned around and said out loud. "Who threw that damn ham at me?"

The entire table laughed so hard. From that moment on, I did a comedy show and before I knew it some had Tears rolling from their eyes as they laughed harder and harder. Being able to laugh took our minds off of the humiliation at inmate intake with the "cough, squat, cough harder humiliation", missing your family, life, death, the unfair sentences, and the system failing some of us. Simply the tears of laughter. The guard looked over at us and smiled to see so many smiles on the inmates faces. I took their minds off of the why does it hurt so bad. Everything doesn't always have to be sad.

Before we knew it, Mrs. Spencer, yelled. "Times up ladies! Line up." We all walked to get into line to follow behind the yellow line.   To watch them wipe tears of laughter from their eyes gave me joy and a feeling of hope.   I would love to perform comedy shows at different prisons around the state and the country, even if I didn't get paid for it.   Regardless, we are still humans, too!

AngieSaidThat.

We walked back into Barrack 19 and a few minutes later my name was called for my appointment in the Law Library.   I quickly rushed to the guard desk eager to go.   As I entered one door another one closed behind me.   Filled with excitement as I walked down the hall, I asked another guard for directions to the Law Library.   I walked in and signed in on the daily log sheets.   I couldn't wait on advice on appeals, or how to file for a sentence reduction, and most importantly, ineffective counseling.   An inmate by the name of Jill, very nicely assisted me with a book on guidelines to filling out forms.

Jill is a white female, 5'4", black hair, brown eyes, cute dimples and very sweet.   I wasn't sure of her charges.   I didn't ask, but she did tell me that a jury trial sucks and that she didn't know anything about how the law works.

She pulled out Rule-37 and allowed me to write down helpful information.   I had my supplies, prayed and read through all that I possibly could in one hour.   Every paragraph I saw on ineffective counsel became my focus.   I asked others about all the legal words I didn't understand.   To think by simply not knowing it could cost you twenty-one years of an unfair sentence.   Ugh!

AngieSaidThat

Jo-Jo Taylor's witness testimony was entirely inconsistent with his courtroom testimony.   This is a violation of petitioner due to process of the fourteenth Amendment of the U.S.C.A.   In court identification is not reliable to admissible when prior to trial confrontation was not accurate.

This witness lied so much in court under oath that he had to read over his witness statement to remember what he previously said.

His testimony made no sense and nothing he testified to match the statement he made six months after the crime. Simply a liar!

Nevertheless, my bail was revoked and I got arrested because Jo-Jo Taylor claimed that I threatened him at my girlfriend's job. He clearly told me that let Marty use his Gun in the bank robbery. He even gave me his phone number to call him. I had seen him about seven months prior at the KUM & Go Convenience Store without incident, but now all of a sudden I am a threat to him. Me, a woman, a threat to a 200 plus pound man! He clearly lied under oath when he testified and made this statement.

"I have cameras around my apartment because I am scared of Angela Richardson. She had her niece knock out my window with a brick screaming. "Leave my Aunt Angie alone you liar!" He also testified that he keeps a gun on him when he goes out in public out of fear. He went on to say that after 12-12-12 he stopped working for me and that I paid him $5.00 a night to do security for me at the club. Now, who would be stupid enough to work security anywhere for $5.00 a night? Liar! A witness testified that on New Year's Eve night she rode with Caspar to the club. Jo-Jo didn't even want to return Marty's truck. I text his mother to pick it up after he repeatedly lied about returning the truck. All of this was recorded on the jail house phone calls and I was told that the calls would be played in the courtroom by my court appointed public defender. Of course they didn't play any of the phone calls, but she got paid regardless, remember?

On another day in the Law Library I listened very carefully to an old inmate as she spoke. As I watched her I couldn't help but ask how long had she been here. Miss Grandma Cookie replied back quickly and fancy. "That's none of your business." As she looked over her glasses, in

Her creased white uniform, with a roller set hairdo.   She had class even behind the bars.

"Well ma'am, I'm sorry to have asked you that.   Do you know Yvette?"   I replied.

"Sure, I do." The little old white lady answered with a smile. "Is she a friend of yours? And that's okay about asking me that, but it is still none of your business."

"Yes ma'am.   She's a friend of mine and you are exactly right. I'm sorry."   I apologized with a smile.

After I had read for awhile, Jill looked over at me and asked. "So, you had a jury trial, huh?   This is going to be hard because you cost the state money, even if you didn't know how the system worked.   They are going to keep denying you, but we will keep appealing your case.   It may take some time, but it wasn't fair on sentencing or counsel."   She said.

Directly across from me another inmate was looking at me while she was writing, but she didn't say anything.

"Are you writing an appeal?"   I asked her.

"Yes, this is my third one in a few years.   I've been here for eight years on a capital murder charge."   She explained.

I couldn't help but think of Tupac's lyrics. *"I ain't no killer, but don't push me."*

"Thank you."   I smiled as she explained how appeals worked.   I also received advice from some of the other inmates in white that cared, even if they were not getting paid regardless.

I knew some of these legal books would puzzle my under educated mind, but it is never too late to learn. It's better to know than not to know. If you know better, you do better in life. Another appointment at 8:30 AM in the Law Library and Angela Richardson vs the State of Arkansas in Jesus name.

AngieSaidThat

I returned back to Unit 19 with the knowledge of steps to take to gain my freedom from serving time that should have been equally granted to me on compliance of robbery being that I was the driver and never inside the bank. This railroad feeling had me searching for a train ride crossing these tracks. This train had derailed, but I couldn't stop it or give up on the arrival of a long ride home, even doing the breakdown, change of oil, and brake change. But just wanting to make it was my reason for purchasing a ticket at the stationary section of commissary. My ineffective counsel really drove me in the wrong direction. It excited me when my commissary arrived with my writing supplies. I received my large clasp envelopes, pens, dictionary, four writing pads, and other items. This is my station, my purpose. Where would it take me? Who will care enough after election time to grant me a fair sentence in the state of Arkansas? I wasn't just focused on learning to write an appeal. I'm writing books, mentoring the youth, uplifting spirits with my comedy, and bringing laughter into the lives of the inmates inside these bars. And all in less than two weeks in prison serving a twenty-one year sentence. How amazing am I in the State of Arkansas? I am a gifted writer, a comedian, and spiritually ready. And most importantly, delivered and free of all the "crap" and dice included!

AngieSaidThat

Officer Story continued to call out the mail. I received mail about my Notice of Appeal from the Office of Public Defender marked "Priority".

In the Circuit Court of Pulaski County Arkansas Seventh Division. State vs Angela Richardson, Notice of Appeal.

Dear Mr. Richardson: (Mr. a mistake) A typo on their behalf or was it a joke? Or do they know the truth that it was a male inside the bank with Marty?

Please find enclosed a copy of the original Notice of Appeal filed on your behalf which starts the appeal process on your case. The court reporter now has at least ninety days within which to process the transcript of the trial, but that time can be extended up to seven months. When the transcript is filed with the court of Appeals or the Supreme Court, we will then be given a briefing schedule, which will give us the date your appeal is to be filed.

After we receive the briefing schedule, we will then notify your which attorney will be preparing your brief and that process will be explained to you. Any questions contact me at 201 S. Broadway.

Sincerely,

Deputy Public Defender

Chapter 41

Good Deeds

Notice of Appeal

Comes the defendant, Angela Richardson, who was declared indigent and pray an appeal to the Arkansas Court of Appeals from the conviction and sentence received in the above styled matter at the conclusion of the jury trial proceeding held on June 3, 2014 and the sentencing held on June 3, 2014 and from the resulting sentencing order filed on June 17, 2014 and designates the entire trial record, as his record of Appeal in the case. Also requested are all hearing including, but not limited to March 3, 2014 and May 1, 2014.

Respectfully Submitted

By: Jeannie Copeland
    Deputy Public Defender

So respectfully submitted until I'm Mr. Richardson and as "his" Record of Appeal in this case. But, they "get paid regardless", remember?

Shortly after writing My Wife, Alicia, B'Nutt and my friend Denise, I laid the Notice of Appeal inside the Bible at Psalm 58. The jingling of Officer Story's keys continued to make noise like the sound of the Salvation Army bell ringers at Christmas time. As he made his rounds, he noticed that I was still up writing. A friendly but evil reminder of the long hours up shooting dice, but the thought Of being awake to fulfill my purpose of writing was indeed the friendly part about it.

I figured facing twenty-one unfair and unjustified years in prison for not knowing and not being advised properly about a jury trial and incorrectly sentenced over a gap that wasn't mine was more than enough to motivate me to get an understanding of the law and to fulfill my purpose of writing. I was told by my attorney friend, Stanley, the hour he visited that he really didn't see a gap in the photo. So to be loved by him as he say, the only gap in the world was in my teeth. No one in the world has a gap, but me. This person has a mustache, large yellow teeth, and a bigger gap, but it's me. Now as I read the Notice of Appeal, I am now Mr. Richardson. Just another case closed and they "get paid regardless", remember?

In today's way of living most people need to know that things change. I was told at A.C.I. attending Sunday night services that nothing remains the same, but a tree. We all know there are four seasons in a year. Summer, winter, spring, and fall. Every year the tree will do as those seasons requires.

Even, my appointed counsel didn't know the difference between a cross-dresser and a man that simply covered up in a wig, scarf, and a hat with a soft voice. They never mentioned the man's shoes, pants, or hands. A cross-dresser is a beautiful drag queen that takes out time to look flawless. Most need to take a look at RuPaul Drag race and catch it!

The prosecutor presented a Face book photo of me sitting at the bar of my club with a friend name Valerie and in no way did the picture captured by the bank surveillance camera look anything like me.

After I testified, the jury was convinced that it was me in the photo after they saw the gap in my teeth.

Verdict: Guilty
Sentence: 21 years

Valerie Williams had testified to the truth that Jo-Jo continued to work at my club after 12-12-12 and proved that the court allowed him to continue to lie under oath in court during his entire testimony. My case consisted of a lot of "he say, she say", rather than proven facts. In my series of books this will be proven and revealed by court records.

I now understand why so many people are lost in our justice system. We are not advised properly. We don't fully understand the law and get thrown away as if nothing matters. We end up just another inmate in an overpopulated prison system.

What about the prisoners who were scared into a plea deal because they didn't understand the law and know their rights? They have signed away their rights to appeal as part of the plea deal. A lot of them are unable to read and/or understand just what they are signing.

GOD, please place people into these elected offices that will listen and read the unfairness of our convictions.

Please send fair politicians who care about our rights as well. Their commercials on television speak out to citizens soliciting their votes and most politicians will tell you anything to get your attention and your vote, but a lot of what's really going on doesn't make the campaign ads or television commercials. Like sentencing people to serve 70% of their sentence, which often are unfair sentences to begin with. People if you are able to vote, please be careful of who you elect to hold offices.

As my attorney friend said, "What happens when the horses are out of the gate? Who really cares when they are all running for the finish line?"

Why wasn't there an acknowledgment of all my great community deeds? What really happened to Senator Tracy Steele when he ran for mayor of North Little Rock? The first time he won by the votes, but the horses found away to take another look at the race on screen and of course the wrong horse was in the lead and Senator Steele was scratched out of the race.

Truthfully speaking Tommie Normby, a great North Little Rock police officer, has served our community with nothing but respect. But when he's in uniform helping Tracy Steele it's a problem! And lets not forget that the Chief of Police of Little Rock son killed a fifteen year old black boy and was found not guilty. Is this justice for us all!

My mind took me in a place in which only GOD could feel me. It may not have meant anything to our State Representatives about all the people I have helped and mentored in our community, but most of them have had bad experiences in their lives as well. We are all human. GOD has given them another chance in life and in their occupations.

Anyone is welcome to stop reading my book now and simply sign in to my Face book page, which is still active, to see that my work speaks for itself. My name "AngieSaidThat" is known in various states, not just throughout Arkansas, and no one could believe the verdict and most definite not the sentencing.

Anya, an inmate, could barely walk, and was issued a walker after seeing medical. She damn near fell trying to share an article that was meant for me to read.

*A former McCellan High School coach who killed a friend and maimed a
second person in a drunken driving crash got ten years probation.
Family and friends testified on his behalf of his good work as a mentor to
generations of young men. To send him to jail will compound this
tragedy for a man who has changed lives with positive influence. He
has committed a crime, but he is not a criminal, his attorney argued.*

My mouth dropped opened! The way I have helped our
community by inviting several to church at ACI Awareness, saving
many from committing suicide, talking many into going back to school
or joining the military, speaking to them about practicing safe sex, trying
to help Them to get off drugs, providing a place for them to live (some
lived in the club), and helping them to find a place to live and/or
employment. I have hosted events all over the state and held
fundraisers for various events and people. I have mentored Job Corp
students, and the lists of my good deeds go on and on.

I am the head leader of our black gay community. "The Head
Nitch" to it all. Most clubs refuse cross dressers or they have to argue,
fight, or watch their backs from the thugs and others judging them or
wanting to shoot them. Most of the cross dressers are so beautiful and
are mistaken for real women. I feel for them and I live it with them. I
have argued with other club owners for turning drag queens away from
their clubs because of their lifestyles claiming it's against the law to
come in as a drag queen. They claim they can't protect them from
violence by the other patrons. If you think I am lying, ask B-Level
about when he operated Club Hollywood on Asher Avenue. The club
on the hill doesn't welcome them either, but they were not rude about it.
Now most have changed identities and are considered as women. I see
it in here at prison. Men are considered women after the change.
Some women in here look so much like men that I once turned and put
my nose to the wall. That's the rule in Newport Prison for female
inmates, if men prisoners are walking through the prison hallways to
work. I got AngieSaidThat confused. Ugh!

Most will be surprised by what I have witnessed some of the most beautiful drag queens experience in the straight clubs. I helped other club owners understand that we are people too! Our money is green and spends the same. So, most business owners such as 521, Jazzi's, Trois, and Four Corners understand the profits on a business tip and leave their personal issues within themselves versus judging my people. Even the white gay club owner on Jessie Road. Do I like him? Yes, I love the queen, but I will never forget him asking me, "How do you deal with those people?"

My reply was simple. "I am one of those people." Once he came to my club with a bodyguard to make a donation to a fundraiser I was having for someone and to check it out of course. He missed "those people" currency. It's not personal, it's business. So, why not welcome the gay niggers back? They have been called niggers on Jessie Road, but some will fall for anything. They just think that they deserve to be mistreated by others. Why not stand for something? This is why I am up all night and all day mostly writing.

I know that if you don't stand for something, you will for anything! I stand!

AngieSaidThat

Why wasn't either of my Face book pages acknowledged in court or treated equally? Both of my Face book pages, Angie S. Richardson and AngieSaidThat are filled with posts of my great community services. Some people are dead, but I get twenty-one years over a gap that wasn't mine!

All I can do is SMH, (shake my head) and think about Psalms 58. Judge Piazza is truly for same sex marriages and equality. All I can say is this to the many that will read this book. Please vote for those that care and not for those that know and perform like they are getting paid regardless, as my court appointed public defender told me, and trying to make something look good around election time. Some of these public defenders really could care less about the outcome of the cases. The paid attorney will defend and make it happen just like the attorney did in the verdict of the high school coach.

The system of the State of Arkansas failed me and plenty of others, but I'm taking it to the Supreme Court if I have to.

I'm currently in Newport Prison. I didn't have $10,000.00 for a private attorney just like most of us can't afford a private doctor. However, in 2008 someone who understood due to living life and not just from hearing about it or reading it on the news feed cared enough for change. President Obama.

AngieSaidThat

This is not my battle. I have been advised by my spirit to take my steps toward the mountain and he can and will move it. My faith and hope is stronger than any verdict form twelve people that couldn't possibly understand the lifestyle of gays nor the law.

Over seven years I hosted Black Gay Pride and freely feed over three hundred people out of my own pocket. I have sponsored Arkansas Queen boat cruises, hosted stopped the violence comedy shows and held stop the bullying meetings, but probation for causing a death for a football mentor.

Is there a difference between a person with an alcoholic drinking addiction and a person with a gambling addiction breaking the law?

Is there a difference between a gay mentor with the youth and an ex-football coach straight man that mentors the youth?

Chapter 42

My Office Chair

Saturday evening sitting in a corner in a small area in all white, my mind took me there, yes there! I thought about my Mama listening to the song by Gladys Knight as she was driving to the races as well as other great and blessed memories of my Mama. I missed my Mama. I wouldn't have ever been sitting in here in all white if she were still living. I couldn't help but think of the all white Mother's Day event I sponsored by cruising the Arkansas River with over one hundred people aboard the "Mark Twain". I enjoyed the cruise and I miss many of the people who were there.

Minutes later I walked in the room to grab a soda that was as hot as summer piss after two seconds in a microwave. We are lucky to taste ice if it's served in the chow-hall. Ice was the only thing 3201 W. Roosevelt had that wasn't bad. How I wish some could have remained frozen in my Bible. I returned to the most comfortable chair in Unit 19 at the desk that was actually for the forms that the inmates must fill out to request anything from medical to laundry. You are out of luck if a form is not filled out correctly. I neatly placed all the forms on the corner side of the table. The inmates started calling it Angie's office and allowed me to have it every time returned.

Well, one particular time a young white stud, who was probably about twenty-five years old with black hair, pretty teeth, brown eyes, 5'4", and about 165 lbs sat down in the chair and then got up to talk to her girlfriend.

"Hey, let me sit there till you come back. I will give the chair back to you." I said.

I was writing earlier until the guard called for chow. Sometimes, I will talk to the guard about my book. She will say, "Richardson, I didn't make my hourly round. Don't move until I finish listening." The feeling of the feedback is simply amazing.

Truly understand this. I never felt the spirit of GOD's presence and favor so close to me. My body, soul, and mind are being soaked with motivational powers of wanting to uplift and mentor others. Even with the young stud that wanted the chair. Dressed in her all white uniform thinking she's a man. Bullies in prison!
"Hey, Angie, you better give me my chair back! You left and have been in your room. So, if you get up you no longer have the right to the chair unless no one is sitting in it." She said standing over me.

I looked up at her without smiling. I had just heard this little "she/he" talking about going to Tucker Boot Camp. The way she said it wasn't cool at all. She wasn't about that life as my people say.

"Look, playa, that is not the way you ask me for this chair back by demanding it. I respect everybody in here and by all means don't allow the little wanna be man role in you to have me giving you this chair back in a way that we both probably wouldn't agree to. And if you are so much of a man, then take it back." I said to her without smiling or taking my sexy eyes off of her.

"I'm not going to "Seg" and get locked down over this chair." She replied. The sound of her voice reminded me of the oldies, but goodies country songs.

Actually, I wasn't tripping over the chair. I was sleepy and had dozed off during count time and jumped up knowing my pen and paper were still out there on the table. I had planned on just getting it and returning to sleep. Plus, I had been up all night writing and not to mention Mr. Story, the guard, shook my room down in search of his missing ink pen at 6:00 AM. Ugh!

So, I was already irritated and sleepy and then she was out of order. She didn't care about how she talked to anyone. It's not as if I pretend to be the big bad wolf, but the bullies in prison will try certain people. But not AngieSaidThat!

Shamed, she walked off after I read her into a coma and as sleepy as I was I never moved out of the chair on the strength that she will do someone else like that if I didn't stop her. She was even taking a chance of being kicked out of the strict boot camp at Tucker Boot Camp with a mouth like hers.

I watched her go tell her girlfriend and three other women that came in from the county jail in her hometown of Russellville, Arkansas, what had happened.

I promise you none of them had the guts to say anything to me about the chair, not to mention two of the women were attracted to me. They knew I wasn't the type to look for trouble, but will hold my own. Respect gets everybody's attention and I have already so soon earned everybody's respect. True enough some could have whipped me, even in my own club, but they respected me, even the ones who disliked me for barring them from my club. Respect is earned, not demanded my people.

This situation reminded me of this little stud, Manish, in Little Rock. She bullied a lot of people. A lot of the younger studs feared her. But the times I barred her, the threats never stopped. She pulled out guns on others, hit them with bricks, shot up their cars, but never raised a hand to me. Our love surpassed what no one in the entire community will ever be able to understand or relate to. She never shot anyone in my spot. Respect plays a major role.

However, about an hour later, I called the stud to the side and explained to her that it wasn't about the chair, but her way of speaking to others wasn't cool. I also told her she wouldn't make it in boot camp with a mouth like that. After we talked she thanked me and I smiled as I gave her The chair back. We have been cool every since. We often check on each other and sometimes shoot basketball together. I'm sure she is going to do great in boot camp and be more mindful of how she speak to others.

I couldn't help but make everyone crack up laughing about the guard, Mr. Story, searching my room.

"Richardson, step outside of your room." He demanded.

My cellmate and I stepped outside the door. I'm thinking, really over an ink pen? I'm about to get another two years or more added to my sentence. If a gap got me twenty-one years, surely a guard's ink pen will get me even more. I watched him search my blankets and sheets. He went under the mattress. He opened up my large bag and search through all my food. He searched and searched, but did not find a pen.

"Let me touch your hair." He said joking and laughing.

"So, why am I your suspect, Mr. Story?" I asked.

Mr. Story looked country. No country is an understatement, he looked rodeo style!

"Well, who else stays up all night writing until morning? And you would love to have my pen with some good ink in it like that one, wouldn't you? I see that you Love to write. I have never ever seen anyone in this prison up all night writing. So, yes you are my suspect." He answered.

I smiled and said. "Well, if I find it, I'm going to use all of the good black ink and return it when the ink runs out." We both laughed.

What really happened to Mr. Story's ink pen? Cough harder!

Hours later, after having a little fun laughing and teasing others, I noticed new people coming in the door. All I could think about was the horrible cough and squat procedure. I felt like I had been raped by a motorcycle gang without warning. I knew some of them had been to prison before. One female had returned to prison over eight times. The true facts of all the returning in and out of prison has really made me think of the West Memphis Three. The three men that were locked up for years for a crime they probably didn't commit and later released. The State of Arkansas will make you want to leave the state and never return. They are so far behind on what matters.

I respect the fact that Judge Piazza had the feeling that some things may not ever happen again. He stood up for same sex marriage in our state. But, do most stand for equality and fairness? Hell no!

My trial to place in the courtroom of a judge who is rumored throughout the community to have an alcohol and Cocaine addiction as well as possibly other illegal addictions. I tried to tell the court that Jo-Jo Taylor was lying under oath about me threatening him.

The judge's response was. "He say. She say. The law even breaks the law."

A day later I prayed about all of it. I know most of them will have to answer to a much higher and powerful judge. The State of Arkansas can't possibly think because these people are "getting paid regardless" that they are doing a good job. Even without advising me properly, Mrs. Copeland, was still able to get her bi-weekly paycheck.

Again, had I known about a jury trial and how these people are selected, there would have been no way in hell on a cold day that I would have agreed to a jury trial, regardless of all the rumors and even the judge telling a mutual friend that he would have given me more time if he could. Why? He of all judges should understand the power of addictions. The word "addiction" falls under the umbrella of any kind of addiction, plus I had never been in his courtroom or had any prior convictions. Why? He even ran Marty's charges con-current, but mine are consecutively. Why? Justice can't be the answer. Or fairness either.

Could it be because I stood up for an entire community that needed equality and provided a safe place to allow them to be themselves? I owned a gay club where the police were hardly ever called and there were definitely no killings. We all just wanted, like other people, to be able to go out and enjoy ourselves without the name calling, the Bullying, or even being killed for dressing in the attire of our choice. Even if men wanted to dress like women, we were in our own zone, in our own lane. Enjoying what is known as living and loving life.

I thought about my Mama again and how she explained that everybody loves a winner. How the more money and cars you have, the more friends you are going to have. People will want to be in your life when you are on top. She use to tell me all the time that my heart was too big and too giving and that people do not treat me the same way that I treated them. I didn't understand it then, but I understand it now. I think about how she wanted me to go to college. I stopped writing and looked down at my paper in my all white prison uniform and closed my eyes. I placed my hand on my back as if she was rubbing it with tears in my eyes as I heard the officer's keys making noise.

Mama knew I wasn't going to give up. I will always remember her words. "I'm not worried about you. You are strong like me." I started writing a little faster and invited another inmate, a young lady by the name of Alexis, into what I claimed as my "prisoner interview office".

I poured out the hot orange Big K soda I was sipping on and replaced it with water from the sink in cell# 212. We are not even allowed a bottle of water in prison. Ugh! People please stay out of trouble and be careful of your surroundings. I know so many in Arkansas listens as I speak. This is not where you want to be. It is today's new slavery with all races. Government has become the Whipping boy. Our youth are at risk if we don't get involved. The world has changed and some of those laws can't remain the same. Our people are worth more as prisoners than college students seeking an education.

Chapter 43

Alexis

It would be a shame for me not to tell anyone about the mosquitoes. I grabbed my dictionary that I ordered from commissary to correctly spell the insect that caused my hand to itch.

It reads: *A winged insect of which the female bites and sucks blood of other animals and humans.*

I thought about the messages from the other female inmates and officers warning me to stay on my bunk after intake. I also thought about being moved to the compound as the other inmate talked so excitedly about the cute blond head in Unit 19. Did these mosquitoes also have to squat and cough? They are females and are eating me up already. So, what do the male mosquitoes do to our bodies? Ugh! I thought about someone very special to me, Mrs Washington. She always told me. "You ain't scratching where you're itching?" It depends on where the wings of the female mosquitoes are biting...lol!

My mind wasn't focused on any of the relationships period.   I missed My Wife more than words could ever say.   I replayed memories of her voice inside my head to ease the Pain until she finally get a chance to visit.   I thought about New York during New Year's Eve, watching the ball drop as another blessed New Year rolls in.   I have never been to New York.   I watched a lot on television about the places I imagined taking her.   I continued writing and thinking about laying my lips softly on hers at the stroke of midnight.   Thanking her for loving me unconditionally even while serving prison time.

Quickly, I came out of my fairy tale and back to the reality of sitting in prison and far from New York.   With this unjustified time, will I ever be able to take her?

Biting down on the side of my lip again, my Mama's voice and a vision of her face crossed my mind.   I needed GOD to order a phone up in heaven.   Just to hear her voice one last time is all I needed.   Or is it all I need was for my mind to be free?   I picked up my soda can filled with water and looked away so no one could see the tears that had formed in my eyes.

Alexis Sims, Inmate# 71264

She followed me over to the table after only two days of coming to prison.   We talked briefly and as always my personality was opening up something within her in which I can't seem to understand and probably never will.

Alexis is 5'3", 206 lbs, brown hair with blonde streaks, thick eye brows, brown eyes, and hair on her face.

"How are old are you?" I asked.

"Thirty-three." She answered

"Where are you from?" I asked.

"I'm from Searcy, Arkansas." She answered.

"Why are you here?" I asked.

"I'm here for murder." She stated and grabbed my arm to stop me from writing.

"Angie, I can't believe that I'm talking to you. So many of my friends have been to your club. I must tell you the truth, the victim was my mother." She said while rubbing my arm.

I stopped writing and dropped my pen looking her eye to eye. Her eyes looked like eyes on a pair of dice. We as gamblers called them "snake eyes." I cannot explain to anyone the way my stomach felt. Great America, Six Flags, or the Arkansas State Fair rollercoaster ride would be an Understatement. My heart damn near skipped beating. Tears formed in my eyes thinking about my own Mama.

How many of us wish our own mothers were still here and I'm sitting with someone whose hand remained on my arm that killed her only Mama.

"Hold on, let's pray before we start talking about what happened. I stated.

I prayed amongst the four of us. "Lord, guide us as I write this story. It's not going to be easy. Please forgive us all for even being here. Allow me to open up my heart and listen to this young lady who needs my listening ear. I ask these things in your name, Jesus." And we all agreed and said, "Amen."

Alexis continued. "its complex what led to this night. I want to tell my testimony to you. I'm bi-racial and all my life I have really had it hard from the white side of my family. They raised me and loved me, but they don't like black people." She explained. "Even on the outside with their smiles, they are fake. I remember one day my grandfather came home after he had been drinking. I was in college and had come home tired from classes. He told me it was my fault that my mama didn't have a good life." She continued. "I was the backbone for my family. I will never forget how my aunt allowed her husband to molest their two year old baby girl and his nine year old step-daughter. I would babysit my cousins during the summer and felt bad about the family secrets." She said.

"So, tell me about the night that you killed your mother. I also want to come back to the family secrets. I don't understand." I said.

The officer screamed. "Chow time."

Alexis looked me deep in the eyes and asked. "Angie, will you eat with me?"

"Do you really want me to?" I asked.

"Yes, I do." She answered.

"Okay." I said.

We all formed a line and walked down the hall behind the yellow line. I can't lie and tell you that it wasn't on my mind. I couldn't eat for thinking about the person whose cup I carried to the table. Alexis killed her mother? Why, when, where, how? Minutes later we walked back over to the desk by ourselves. I wanted to be with Alexis alone to get the details of her story.

"Alexis will you finish telling me your story, please?" I asked.

"I got to tell you what happened. I'm trying to figure out why." She said. "It was dry around town and no one had any ice, but me. The dude I was messing with hit me in the head with a pistol because he needed some dope. He threatened to kill me and Mama. I dropped him off and put some dope in my hiding place. I later went to Little Rock off of 12th Street to the dope house, but I didn't see any familiar cars, so I didn't stop. I told my Mama I needed to go to the hospital. I drove back to Searcy a few hours later and stopped by my Mama's job. She worked at Big Lots, but she wasn't ready to get off yet. I saw the money handler dope boy at her job pretending like he needed a job. He was talking to Mama as he was holding an application in his hand. It all seemed weird to me. Later, I went back after the police were called about something to do with some threats and a missing I-Phone. He and a few others were pissed off because I moved a lot of dope and whenever they ran out I always had it hidden. I had chickens put up." She explained.

"Alexis, what the hell are chickens?" I asked. "Damn, we just had that in the chow-hall."

"Two eight-balls. Two quarter halves of meth." She answered. "Mama had been asking me all night to give her a little more time at work. I sat in my new 2013 truck that I had just got and waited in my pajamas and Ugg boots thinking about the dope boys. My Mama had become so secretive. She had even sat her lap top up to where it took fingerprints in order to get onto it. We argued and I threatened her sometimes. I no longer trusted her. She came out of the store and walked to my truck and cursed me out about the drama on her job." She continued.

"Did you even ask her if she knew about the guy on her job pretending he was seeking a job? Were you on drugs?" I asked.

"No and no." She answered. "She turned to walk off and I shot her." She said staring me in my eyes.

"Did you ever get out of your truck?" I asked.

"No." She answered.

"Did you shoot your Mama in the back?" I asked.

"I don't know. I used three guns on her." She answered.

"What the hell! Why? Just tell me, I don't understand." I asked as chills formed all over my body.

"I felt like she knew something. I didn't trust her." She said.

"What type of guns did you use?" I asked.
"The Judge, which is two guns in one. It's a 45 and a rifle held together and I used a 25 caliber pistol. It took her a few seconds to fall." She said looking directly at me.

I stopped and prayed again. I closed my eyes and asked GOD to guide my pen as I continued

"Alexis, OMG, what did you do afterwards?" I asked.

"I drove off, but after a few seconds I went back. I just snapped, but I wanted Mama to be okay. I vomited on myself. I asked her to get up. Mama please, Mama get up!" She started crying as she continued.

"Why didn't you kill the person that hit you in the head with the pistol and the money handler? Why did you kill your very own Mother?" I asked.

"I couldn't trust her, Angie. She told my family that she was afraid that I would end up like my Dad. He killed his Mama at the age of thirty-three years old. He told Mama while serving time that he was going to kill her when he got released from Tucker Max Prison. This happened here in Newport, Arkansas. He shot his Mama with a rifle. My dad told me to move away from my Mama at a certain age, but I didn't listen. I planned on moving to Texas. At one point my half brother on my Dad's side was in the same prison with our Dad for cutting a man's throat. My half brother is dead now. He sold drugs and at the age of twenty he was shot by a police officer right here in Newport." She explained with tears in her eyes.

"So, at the age of thirty-three you took your Mama's life too?" I asked.

"Yes, I did." She muttered.

"What type of time is your Dad doing?" I asked.

"Life plus fifty years in Cummings Prison." She answered.

"Damn!" I said and asked. "How did the police find you and were there any witnesses?"

"Yes, two at Big Lots. The police set up a road block and stop stick tracks to flatten my tires. I ran over them and sled to the right. I kept sliding and hit a deer. The police surrounded my truck with guns everywhere and screamed.

"Get out on your knees and place your face on the ground."

"One of the guns I used on Mama was in my boot and the other one I thought I had thrown it in the river. One belonged to Mama. Angie, I thought she was going to snitch on me. The Feds were in Searcy, but I gave her plenty of dope money. I helped pay her way through Harding University. She received her degree. My grandfather hated the fact that she didn't marry a white Architect instead of a nigger. She wanted to send me away again. I will not accept a snitch or being in a crazy house. I can remember the look on Mama's face. It's like a voice told me to pull my guns on her. She looked at me as if she was in shock and I shot her. I snapped!" She cried, I cried, we cried.

I explained to her that a small word by the name of cancer overpowered my Mama and how badly I wished she was here. I know my gambling addiction started severely after her death. I wanted to give up and I really didn't care about life anymore. I really couldn't understand the fact of her killing her Mama. I couldn't understand it even as she tried to explain it to me. I still do not and never will. I told Alexis it wasn't about me, but she will have to answer to GOD one day. She rubbed on my leg with tears rolling down her face.

"I bet you look a lot like your Mama." I asked.

"Angie, I am so sorry I put you through this." She said.

She cried. I cried tears I couldn't stop them from rolling down my face as I thought of my Mama, who was my hero.

Alexis walked to her room to get a picture of her Mama. Donna Smith, fifty years old, reddish brown hair, 5'3", 135 lbs, top heavy, slim at the bottom, and a beautiful smile. She stood in the photo next to her baby girl, Alexis, who was about six years old with pretty caramel skin, beautiful hair, brown eyes, and the same exact smiles.

"Why didn't you get your gap fixed before court?" She asked. "But you are sexy with it." She said and we both laughed.

While spending time with Alexis, she wanted to sit under me for hours telling me about how the other inmates wanted to get to know me. She continued to tell me about the lifestyle of drug life and about her drug usage.

Four days later Alexis was moved to SPU, the Special Program Unit. I helped her pack outside her door. She smiled with those red, light skinned cheekbones as she watched me carry her bunk mat over my shoulder slowly downstairs and walk back upstairs to grab her bag with the rest of her items.

"What else do you handle like that?" She asked and we both laughed. She thanked me for allowing her to open up and freely talk to me. I hugged Alexis and kissed her on the cheek. I told her to pray about it all. The point being that my judgment days are long gone. GOD holds that position at all times. She killed her mother and I listened on the strength of me trying to help her. Will I understand it? Never! Alexis and GOD will have to handle this on her Judgment Day.

To be sitting in Newport Prison amongst so many in white, but I am a true believer in GOD's will. Up above in the winter skies the wind whispers;

From your skin shines light and everlasting love. You're the man I hoped you would be. When darkness falls I fill with fear, but quickly it all disappears; for I remember when I became still no matter what troubles or dangers cross my path, I know I am guided by my GOD.
He will never leave or forsake you.
This is the mystery of GOD's work.

The thoughts of Alexis raced in my mind faster than a speeding train on a well oiled railroad track, but slower than a handicapped turtle over the fact of killing her Mama. So much of what she shared with me I couldn't get out of my mind. She even admitted she sold drugs to the son, one of our elected highly paid state officials. The son has an addiction and the elected politician sent him away to get cleaned up while he was running for election. I am not willing to mention any names or what takes place during the days and nights while someone is in the midst of a drug addiction, but I know in my heart we are all capable of an addiction. I'm not trying to judge the young man, but his Dad should understand addictions.

I am in deep thought wondering if her Mama ever imagined it as she signed her $100,000.00 life insurance policy listing Alexis, her only child, as the beneficiary that she would be the one to take her life. Her baby girl that looked so adorable in the photo she showed me.

I asked Alexis. "Did you want to go to your Mother's home going services?"

"Yes, I did want to attend. I heard my Grandpa played country music and I know my Mama turned over in her grave. She didn't care for country music. My family wanted me to get the Death Penalty. A few wanted less sentencing." She muttered.

Chapter 44

Generational Curse

Regardless of how large the study is or how impressive the findings are the unresolved questions of why Alexis killed her mother remains. Even in prison Alexis was able to keep thirty Amlodipine, four packs of Omeprazole, thirty Metoprolol, thirty Spironlactone, thirty Furosemide and must report to pill call three times a day for a large amount of other prescribed medications. She is like a zombie. Shortly afterwards I overheard one of the guards in the chow-hall say.

"She is a retard and she killed her Mama."

Another guard told me her brother witnessed it and one of her aunts was a good friend of hers and because Alexis was imprisoned here, the aunt was now working at another prison. True enough our crimes are public record, but what about these rich people who are able to cover up their crimes which have not been reported in big, bold letters in the newspaper. Some "retards" just don't get caught.

By far, I don't agree with Alexis' crime regardless of her reason for killing her Mama. Thinking about Alexis, her Dad, her brother, and all the racism she suffered all of her life from family and friends led me to do all I could do for Alexis.   Read the Bible and pray for her.

Psalm 51:4
Against You, You only, have I sinned,
And done this evil in your sight—
That you may be found just when you speak,
And blameless when you judge.

Is Alexis cursed?   She admitted to me that she believes there is a curse on her father's side of the family.   Negro killers of parents.   I wonder if she had had a child would that child have later killed her. Deep thoughts with injections of the truth!

AngieSaidThat

Chapter 45

Butterflies

Psalms 119:71
The suffering you sent was good for me,
For it taught me to pay attention to your principles.

Sometimes GOD tests us with suffering. Thinking of suffering or woundedness can bring great renewals and healing.

Yesterday we were allowed to go outside for an hour of activity time. I was so thankful to feel GOD's fresh air and nature splash on my skin. I slowly walked around the yard to simply think behind these gates. I needed to talk to Jesus. He experienced prison life. I thought about Paul, but Brother Paul repeatedly came back. I knew in my heart this was it for me. I would never come back to prison!

Out of nowhere, I spotted a beautiful lime green and yellow butterfly. I thought about how Mama loved butterflies. Spiritually I

Knew this butterfly was my Mama unable to talk to me, but sent to me by GOD.

Seriously missing my mother caused tears to roll from my eyes, just like they are now as I write this. I asked the butterfly to please stop. To land those wings. A few feet away from me the beautiful butterfly landed on top of a dandelion. I kneeled down on my knees and asked the butterfly about my two sisters in heaven as tears gently rolled down my face. The other inmates were busy playing softball or talking. No one ever has to tell me how powerful GOD is! He can do exceedingly abundantly above all that we can imagine or say. The power of my Creator sent this beautiful butterfly to me in the spirit of my Mama to let me know that everything was going to be alright. My first visit was so powerful and there was no need for an approval for visitation! This was the best day of my imprisonment.

I walked over to the bench where a beautiful young lady by the name of Crystal was listening to her MP3 player. I plugged in my ear bugs craving for music.

"Were you over there praying?" She asked.

"Yes, with a butterfly and thinking of my Mother." I answered. We continued to listen to Monica's, *"You Are Everything to Me"*. I remembered Kyna lip-syncing it and *all over my body.* I thought about my life in all white and my promise to My Wife.

Please let me make one thing perfectly clear right now. I am not writing this for sympathy. Finally I am my own person, free from it all, and have a feeling of greatness about myself. As you can see, I have made choices in my life, mostly good and some bad which have lead me here.
One thing I learned for sure is that curiosity kills the cat, but not people.

Clearly, most folks have questions about AngieSaidThat. But no one can tell it like me. I dealt with a diverse community and one thing I do know about life is there is laughter and learning. I can't laugh about 12-12-12, but I am learning. Even as a great comedian I know that laughter cannot relieve some pain and emptiness. I had a darkness inside of me, my addiction to gambling. Now I am wiser and I realize that facing reality is the first step to overcoming any addiction.

Don't fight the feeling. It's hard to explain, but it is real. AngieSaidThat is serving time in Newport Prison and will write my own Appeal.

I strongly advise any of my homosexual peers in the LGBT community to stay out of trouble and be fully aware of your surroundings. It only takes a split second to make a wrong decision that will change your life and the lives of others. It only takes one bad decision to fill you with many regrets. For a lot of our young men, both black and white, this is a new form of slavery. As far as the women are concerned, I can say that in Newport, Arkansas, the white inmate outnumber the black inmates, but truthfully is not about color to me.

To the detective that once asked me. "Are you a fucking racist?" I can honestly say that racism isn't my issue. I love people! I dislike the ways of some black people and some white people. But not because of the color of their skin. I dislike the unfairness of June 3rd & 4th, 2014.

To all the people that "get paid regardless" if you do your job effectively or not, I now realize that it is just a job to you.

Chapter 46

Piola

*B*y nurturing my thoughts, I was asked by another inmate, Piola, to read something.

Piola, is 5'4", 145 lbs, cold beautiful black hair, brown eyes, dimples, and with Spanish accent.   She is a very beautiful young lady.

"Angie, you must read this."   She said.

According to the mysteries," A" was the first letter designed by GOD.   Its sound is necessary to breathe out the other letters.   It is an element of air and is called a mother letter because it is one of the basic elements of our creation.   Adam did not become a living soul until GOD breathe into his nostrils and gave him the breath of life.   The lesson of "A" is that of self control.   "A" represents the creative principle, the trio of will, wisdom, and activity.   "A" also stands for ambition.   In a name it adds strength to character.   The "A" wants to be in charge.   "A" stands for aggressive.   So out of ten children, Mama named me Angela.

Most call me Angie and now AngieSaidThat. GOD shows favor, even with the letter "A". Thinking Appeal Granted to Angela…Only GOD!

I'm currently in Newport Prison, but feel to free to write and pray for my appeals. My purpose of writing, comedy, and mentoring will continue with the 12-12-12 Stories of Behind the Bars. Even with my granted appeals I will continue to freely listen to "The Cries Behind the Bars."

AngieSaidThat

Special note from Piola,

I am very confident in that your book will open people eyes and touch many hearts. Writing has become so natural with you and that's what makes it even better. A very real, eye-opening, page turner and a breath taking book. Read Psalms 25, 91, & 59.

Piola is currently serving twenty years for aggravated robbery. She only have to do 3 ½ years. She robbed a man after he won $20,000.00 at the Casino who wanted to have sex with her. She cut his face open. She can't believe my sentencing. It's not fair, but I have been told you can't undo what has been done in our state, but an inmate did twelve years and is now employed here. So, Monica Lewinsky, isn't the only one doing favors under the table. Sounds like "do me Bill" fixed it and got re-elected. Did the media air that during election? So, I believe in the power of prayer and I have faith in GOD and I will be elected.

I jumped off my bunk thinking the officer called for bedtime snacks on my first night in prison. When I got to the area I realized they had actually called for diabetic snacks, but another inmate offered me her Little Debbie in the shower. Just kidding…LOL!

~ Who am I? ~

I am just a person that was overtaken by a small pair of objects that clearly contain "snake eyes".

I am the one that's able to hold together a community that most politicians will really never be able to relate to.

I am the one who held creative AngieSaidThat events for the LGBT community that the politician should have attended instead of making a point around election time.

I am the one to help our community to come up with ideas that will be profitable for us all.

I don't need a vote from the citizens. I need a fair, equal, and a justice reduced sentencing.

AngieSaidThat

Readers, I don't know what you all believe in, but I believe in the power of the Spirit. I really feel sorry those that do not believe in a higher power. On June 4th, 2014, the conviction of having a gap got me an overbite of a sentence in the State of Arkansas. I can only imagine what they have said about me now.

Did the verdict convict a criminal or a powerful mentor, a true blessing to others? I somewhat feel sorry for the public defenders. They have a difficult job with too many calls and too many people to deal with. Making deals and decisions with the prosecutors and judges that will change people's lives forever. Not to mention not having a jury of your peers.

After the 12-12-12 nightmare, I got an invite to perform in a comedy show in Chicago, Illinois, the windy city. *"The Taste of Chicago"*. I would have loved to have given them a taste of

Comedian AngieSaidThat, but due to the fact that it was a few weeks before my trial I couldn't take the offer.

To be honest, I really had second thoughts about the club business. I did it for several years and the fact is the City of Little Rock made it entirely too hard for the clubs on Asher Avenue. It is not that people are killed at clubs. Homicides in Little Rock, Arkansas, have always been on the rise. Why is that? What scare me are closed minded people harassing drag queens.

What can be done to help other club owners on Asher Avenue? Due to the fact that we are not located in the River Market and are all black club owners we do not receive the same treatment. Now, is this fair? No, but who really cares because they will "get paid regardless", remember?

We all know that crimes happen in the River Market, but most of the time it is never reported in the news or on Face book. However, if something happens on Asher Avenue, it makes bold print headlines. The owners of the clubs on Asher Avenue are at fault for everything. We avoid calling the police if something should happen because once the report is made it is eventually held against your business and the ABC (Alcohol Beverage Control Board) gets involved. First, you have to get harassed by Narcotic Agent, Billy Bully, and his crew repeatedly. He made it his business to involve his buddy, the Fire Marshall, to mess with you about the capacity in your club interfering with your crowd.

All of this harassment only takes place on Asher Avenue, but the detective had the audacity to ask me if I am a racist. I think we can all see who the real racists are!

Some may ask why there was a need for a black gay night club. It makes more sense to have a safe place for us to go. It makes sense to have a place where we can freely be ourselves. It makes sense to have a place where we can express ourselves through our

Dress attire.   It makes sense to have a place where we can enjoy music
 And lip syncing shows, some of the best lip syncing shows in the State
of Arkansas, took place at 3910 Asher Avenue.   It makes sense to have
a place where we can feel comfortable in our surroundings, versus, going
to other clubs that deny cross dressers and our safety.   At other clubs of
it is ladies night the stub women are expected to pay admission just like
the men to enter.   The cross-dressers that look flawless as women are
also expected to pay the admission of men.   "Equality".

I did what no one else was able to do and will be what no one else
could ever be, AngieSaidThat.   My events and creations were
untouchable.   It is not about being gay, it's about acceptance of being
who I am and allowing us to be us!

Do I regret leaving the club business? Yes, somewhat, because
we need a place for the black gay community. Do I miss it now?   No! I
did it out of love and because I cared so much for people that I now
realize used me to the fullest.   I now realize that I was too personal
versus business.   My friend, Kim, tried to get me to see that these people
were not truly my friends.   I see know that she was right all along. I
didn't appreciate her then, but I really appreciate her now.   No other
club opened for repast, held fundraisers for burials, provided free food,
back to school supplies drives, and had the cheapest drinks in town.   No
other clubs gave free admissions or half off prices, free VIP, or free road
trips.   I treated my people the way I wanted to be treated, even those
with court cases pending.   I was there for them.   I wrote them and put
money on their books, the same as I did for Marty.   But the prosecutor
used that against me in court, just like the people coming to my club used
me.   But one thing I know for sure is that GOD knows my heart as well
as this purpose!

Psalm 25:18
Feel my pain and see my trouble.   Forgive all my sins.

Trouble is an inevitable by-product of fallen human life. I know the good advice I give to others and my success belongs to me. My writing gift is from GOD and is better than gold. I listen to my Counsel to become wiser. Doing wrong is a fool with an addiction. Wise words of understanding comes from my sexy lips. A wink at the wrong person can cause trouble, but a bold reproof promotes peace. Who is the ultimate role model? Ask what Jesus has done for me. He allowed my dear friend, Vona, to help me understand and find my purpose in life.

AngieSaidThat!

I wonder will my Public Defender, Mrs. Copeland, enjoy my book. My generation will be mentored for the sake of staying out of trouble. Life awareness on all subjects and matters. I want to and will protect them as I would my first born. And it's not just about "getting paid regardless." David protected his sheep and I will protect the LGBT.

AngieSaidThat

Psalm 119:52
I meditate on age-old laws.
Oh Lord, thy comfort me.

I will continue to give to our community and food to the hungry. The Lord free prisoners. He frustrates the plan of the wicked. I can't stand against his freezing cold, but I will stand for fairness on sentencing. I must praise him for his mighty work on my appeals. In Jesus name. Amen.

My purpose through it all is to write and teach people wisdom and discipline on how to do what's right and fair.

I must acknowledge that within my first two months between jail and prison my mind and my addiction were in a great healing place. No one knows how it felt to be in the courtroom standing alone against three men, three gay men at that if I may add. Fink Tillery, the police impersonator. Marty, who flipped on me to protect his lover. Jo-Jo, a big liar, who was under the influence and direction of the police impersonator.

The police impersonator received a degree in Criminal Justice after being released from prison for murder. Without him advising and coaching Jo-Jo on what to say, he would not have been able to remember one lie that he had stated prior to testifying and lying under oath. All three of them got with Marty's mama and his Attorney, Willie Pecker, and changed the entire story. I am not the only one with a gap, but I am without a mustache which was obvious in all the photos in the captured surveillance video inside the bank.

I even called a Sergeant with the Little Rock Police Department, who I know witnessed the blue police light in Fink's, the police impersonator, Impala on a trip to Memphis. However, he never reported anything. I guess it is not always good to say anything to those that are "getting paid regardless."

I was told that the police impersonator got scared and Jo-Jo took the blue police light out of his Impala and now he is delivering pizzas. I was asked if I knew the difference between a pussycat and a delivery driver. A driver can smell it, but he can't eat it. So, as he always said to me. "Eat it queen."

To all the ones listed above, because of the sinful things they say, because of the evil that's on their lips, let them be captured by their pride, their curses, and their lies. My enemies come out at night impersonating the police and flashing a blue wanting the flesh of young men. Snarling like vicious dogs on the prowl of the streets.

But as for me, I am asking the Lord to laugh at them as he rescues me with a reduced sentencing. This I ask in Jesus name and with favor from my Creator. I am blessed with the success of writing with a purpose. Angiesaidthat!

~ shout outs ~

Now finally in closing with prayers, AngieSaidThat must give shout outs to the following;

First of all, shout out to all those that ever came out to support my events at Club Goodtimes at 3910 Asher Avenue. I have very special memories and I love you all. Stay out of trouble!

Shout out to Frank Whitmore
(Watch the Flow) Love you, Frank Jr.

Tee Warren, yes, Doll Baby! I know you couldn't put the book down. Tell San and Sonta to get a copy so y'all can gossip. I miss you guys. See you soon…watch the flow!

Shout out to power people with purpose:

Glam, Nae, Prin, OG Rachel, all the club owners on Asher Avenue, Big Doe, Chicken King, Four Corners, 521, CBM, 101.1, 106.3, Teresa Baker, Randi Carr, Miss Mary, BBR, and all my flawless drag queens.

Shout out to all my comedian buddies:

JRich, Playa Mook, Keef, Lil Jay, Big Dre, Nath, Big Sonia, Wide Load, Blindside, and Superstar Jones.

Laughter to Freedom

I love and miss you guys! What is a man to do in a situation like this?

Pray for me!

Comedian AngieSaidThat

To the State of Arkansas due to the fact of my appeal 800-44, 800-60 Petition: Motion for Reconsideration and Reduction of Sentence, I Angela Richardson is asking Permission to host a Community Comedy Event at the State Capitol or prison of the State's choice.   I also ask that I be allowed to mentor Little Rock Job Corp students along with the LGBT community speaking on awareness.   If in fact I am granted permission to perform a comedy show all proceeds can go to the State of Arkansas on my behalf to pay for the jury that was not of my peers.   Due to the fact of my ignorance of the law and not knowing, no prior convictions, great community service and leader, and most of all cured from a gambling addiction, my time should be reconsidered and reduced to a fair sentencing from the State of Arkansas.   I deserve fairness and I want justice.

Angela Richardson
AKA AngieSaidThat

Most may say that I am crazy, but I am simply amazing

Words From the Author Angela Richardson AKA "AngieSaidThat"

I don't know anyone that has been unfairly sentenced to twenty-one years in prison and has the presence of mind, the passion, and the spirit to write a book in less than two months of incarceration. GOD showed favor by simply allowing me to find the meaning of my purpose in life.

I have done it all. Club owner, comedian, mentor, etc., but not what he has truly planned for me. GOD doesn't shoot dice, not that I'm judging, I'm just speaking on my behalf. He had another plan for me to win without stressing about the next dollar or being involved in a foolish crime. It wasn't me. GOD knows our hearts. Satan feed our spirits of addictions.

Most think I am lying about my learning disability. Just go to the Ole Main High School and look at my transcript. People, when GOD has his favor on you, it's not about your Learning disability or any other problem you may have. What GOD has for you is for you and no one can take it from you. He has given you everything that you need. It is already in you. He has placed it in our spirits. Now, we are all blessed with a gift, but just like at Christmas time, it is up to us to unwrap the gift and discover what our purpose in life truly is. Once we realize that purpose, we must use it and live up to that purpose.

I deserved punishment, but I deserve fair, equal, and justified punishment. As a child I had a baby doll in which the arm broke off. I would fix her arm repeatedly, but sometimes I would just leave the arm broken. I looked at my sisters dolls with both arms and realized my doll deserved to be treated fairly too. My point is, I deserve equal justice and a fair sentence on this bank robbery. I wouldn't have my gap fixed in my teeth on a rich day or even with Obama Care. GOD blessed me with this gap. I am not the only person in this world that has a gap and Marty, my co-defendant, knows that.

However, I am the one accused, but GOD has shown me favor. Many of our American brothers and sisters have to take a stand. I couldn't

Challenge the State of Arkansas by myself, but GOD can change them all! I have turned my faith away from people and placed in the good Lord's hands. All my faith and hope is now in my Creator's hands once and forever.

I'm asking for the real picture to be revealed. Those who saw the bank photos know it wasn't me, but a man with a Mustache and a gap in his teeth. I admit I was involved, but only as the driver. I was never inside the bank.

As I continue to write my next book I will prove facts, truths, and lies. Our justice system has failed so many of us, but GOD has the last say. We are all born sinners, we all have committed sins, and some just get caught, while others are not. I thank everyone for the support. Please contact me at The Arkansas Department of Correction, ADC# 712575. I would love to hear from my readers. I will get my time reduced by the favor of GOD. Although Abraham made many foolish mistakes, he was still mightily used by GOD. And he can still use me too!

The battle is no longer mines. It's the Lord's. And there is power in prayer.
Much love,
AngieSaidThat

"You can look me in my eyes and see I am ready for whatever. Anything that doesn't kill you only makes you better. Take my freedom for a moment, but it ain't forever. I got the Spirit of a Gap "A" State."

"Motivation" by T.I.

Coming soon:
More 12-12-12 Series:
Lyfe & Tyme
The Conviction of the Gap
Tri GOD:Now & Later
Spirits of Addictions
Spirits of Addictions (Second Edition)
Hannah's No Bake Cook Book

www.ingramcontent.com/pod-product-compliance
Lightning Source LLC
Chambersburg PA
CBHW070300290326
41930CB00040B/1631